THE COMPLETE

ILLUSTRATED GUIDE TO

Palmistry

★ ★ ★ ★ ★

THE COMPLETE
ILLUSTRATED GUIDE TO
Palmistry

★ ★ ★ ★ ★

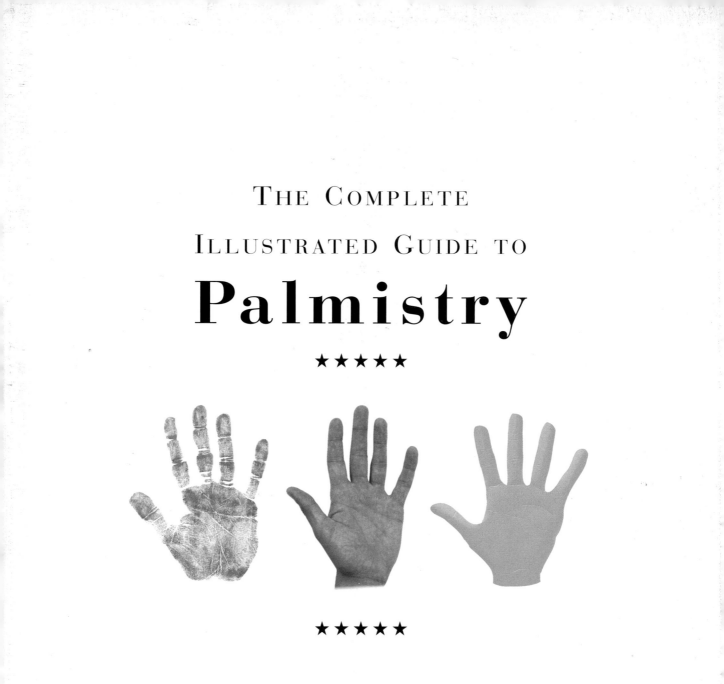

★ ★ ★ ★ ★

PETER WEST

BARNES
&NOBLE
BOOKS
NEW YORK

First published in Great Britain in 1998 by
ELEMENT BOOKS LIMITED
Shaftesbury, Dorset SP7 8BP

This edition published by Barnes & Noble Inc.,
by arrangement with Element Books Ltd

1998 BARNES & NOBLE BOOKS

M 10 9 8 7 6 5 4 3 2

ISBN 0 7607 1179 8

NOTE FROM THE PUBLISHER
Any information given in this book is not intended to be
taken as a replacement for medical advice. Any person with a
condition requiring medical attention should consult a
qualified practitioner or therapist.

Designed and created with
The Bridgewater Book Company Limited

ELEMENT BOOKS LIMITED
Creative Director Ed Day
Managing Editor Miranda Spicer
Senior Commissioning Editor Caro Ness
Production Manager Susan Sutterby

THE BRIDGEWATER BOOK COMPANY
Art Director Terry Jeavons
Designers Jane Lanaway, Stephen Parker
Editorial Director Sophie Collins
Managing Editor Anne Townley
Project Editor Caroline Earle
Picture Research Liz Moore

Printed and bound in Italy

Library of Congress Cataloging in Publication
data available

PICTURE CREDITS

CONTENTS

★ ★ ★ ★ ★ ★ ★ ★ ★ ★ ★ ★ ★ ★ ★ ★ ★

INTRODUCTION

A GIFT FROM THE EAST

★ ★ ★ ★ ★

Strictly speaking, palmistry – divination from the lines and other features of

the palm of the hand – is neither an art nor a science, but a blend of both.

It can perhaps be called an art-science.

As an art form, palmistry is a personal matter, passed down over the

centuries largely by word of mouth from one palmist to another. Since its

beginnings, palmistry has usually been practiced through one-to-

one interviews, with no outside observers. These interviews have

rarely been written down or recorded, and anything we

know about them has usually come from reports given after

the event, often by people who weren't even there. So accurate

histories are virtually nonexistent. It is easy to understand, therefore,

how palmistry's origins and many of the earliest ideas and theories

behind it have become lost or distorted over the years.

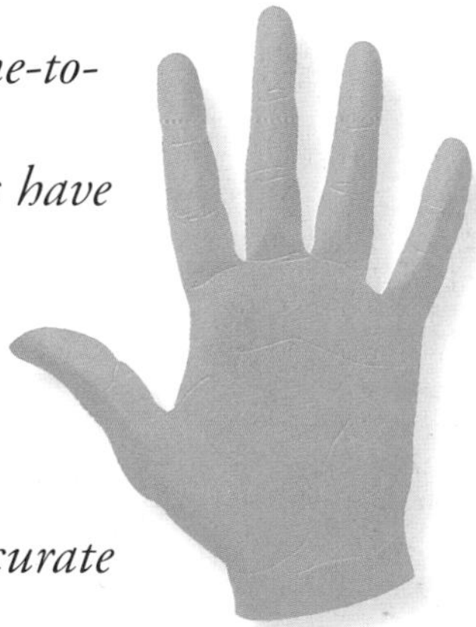

ABOVE The ancient art of palmistry was first practiced thousands of years ago in the East, and most probably originated in India.

Today, although palmistry is still a personal matter, the practice

has a much more scientific background and is informed by modern methods

of observation and reasoned deduction. The original precepts as we have

come to understand them are still there, but palmistry has come of age.

THE BEGINNINGS

* * * * * * * * * * * * * * * * *

THREE MAIN ELEMENTS MAKE up the complete study of palmistry: chiromancy, the study of the lines and other features of the palm; chirognomy, the study of character and personality as suggested by the shape of the fingers, thumbs, and hand; and dermatoglyphics, the study of the skin patterns of the fingers, thumbs, and palms. Because palmistry and palmists are open to suggestion and move with the times, many practitioners now include a fourth element – gesture, the behavioral science of hand and body movement.

RIGHT The palm is divided into zones and marked with the signs of the zodiac in this colorful woodcut illustration from Agrippa's *De Occulta Philosophia* (1533).

Chiromancy is by far the oldest branch of study in palmistry – the ancient palm readers all studied the lines on the hands. However, they generally paid little if any attention to the hand's shape.

Chirognomy came fully into being in the middle of the nineteenth century. The addition of chirognomy to basic chiromancy as an aid to character assessment made a valuable contribution to the accuracy of palmistry.

In the second half of the twentieth century, scientific research into dermatoglyphics led to even greater knowledge and understanding. By adding dermatoglyphics to the other elements palmistry became much more of a comprehensive art-science. It has developed into a refined and reasoned assessment system employed to estimate character, judge talent and capability, define disposition and potential, and verify the health of a subject.

Throughout the world, research into palmistry is continuing. Both China and Japan are at the forefront of new research, as are many of the former Eastern bloc countries. In Great Britain, pioneering experiments conducted in several hospital and university research departments have yielded fascinating results, especially in the sphere of dermatoglyphics.

In many parts of the world, more and more business personnel and recruitment organizations are finding that hand analysis is an invaluable tool in helping place the right people in the right jobs. In fact, there are so many successful hand analysts practicing in the modern business world that they rival astrologers and graphologists, whose own respective talents have only recently become acceptable.

The first part of this book has been designed to allow readers to study and learn the techniques of modern hand analysis. The

BELOW It is possible that palmistry originated in the East. As this statue of Buddha would suggest, the hand and palm are thought to hold great spiritual significance in Eastern religions.

second half, the practical palmistry section, will show how this knowledge can be applied on a day-to-day basis.

No one can say for sure, but palmistry almost certainly came from the East, probably from India. Most of the oldest writings and illustrations, some as much as 5,000 years old, are of Indian origin. There is also evidence from about the same period that palmistry was known in ancient China, Korea, and Japan. It was not until quite some time later that the Western world began to record any knowledge of palmistry. There are some scant early remarks and references from Europe and the British Isles, but most are difficult to date.

In ancient times palmistry was largely superstition, with no hard and fast written rules – anyone could learn it and pass it on as part of traditional lore. Even if there had been rules, very few people could read and write before the 15th or 16th century, so they were probably never recorded. For those who were literate, palmistry would have been low on their list of priorities.

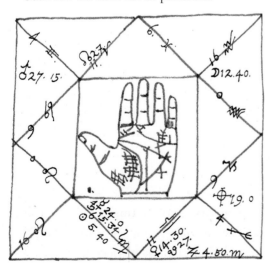

Although there is no documented proof that palmistry was widespread in Greek and Roman times, there are plenty of literary references that suggest it was. In one text, dated as early as 240 B.C.E., it is mentioned that Aristotle was familiar with the subject, and although there is no proof that he did so, he is credited with writing a treatise about palmistry. If Aristotle did write anything at all, the art he referred to was probably ancient even in pre-Christian times.

Early written documentation in English is sketchy, largely because Old English, or Anglo-Saxon, the official written language before 1066, was not standardized throughout the many small kingdoms that made up the British Isles. From around the time of the Norman Conquest in 1066 written Latin began to be used, but only by the clergy – few ordinary people could speak Latin, much less write it.

After 1066, an influx of Norman settlers in Britain caused language problems to arise. The old languages of Britain were not compatible with the new Norman languages,

ABOVE A fortune teller and child are clearly depicted as nomads in this 19th-century painting by Edward Barnes. Palmistry was thought to have been introduced to the West by Gypsies.

LEFT An early map of the hand marked with the horoscope of a birth that took place in Bratislava on August 17, 1567. It illustrated Rothmann's *Chiromantiae Theoretica Practica*.

and direct communication between the two groups proved to be far from easy. Before anything could be written down, it had first to be translated orally from Norman into Anglo-Saxon and then into Latin. Grammar, as we know it today, was nonexistent, and the monks, who still did most of the writing, had no set rules or principles to secure meaning in their written work.

But perhaps the most important reason so little was written about palmistry, or any similar subjects, is that the Church considered hand reading to be the work of the devil. Any such activity was strongly discouraged. In view of all this, it is hardly surprising that we find almost no written records referring to palmistry until the middle of the 15th century, around the time that the printing press was developed.

Indeed, opposition from the established Church, which was extremely powerful, was the biggest obstacle encountered by palmists. The church opposed the practice of astrology too, and as palmistry and astrology were often closely linked, the adherents of both arts experienced oppressive and difficult times.

Still, a few persistent scholars and practitioners managed to contribute to the growth and development of

palmistry. An important advocate was the Swiss Theophrastus Bombastus von Hohenheim, better known as Paracelsus. Born in 1493, the son of a doctor, he is regarded by many to be a fount of occult knowledge. A skilled healer and physician with many recorded cures to his credit, Paracelsus was also a gifted numerologist and astrologer. It is widely thought that he learned palmistry from the wandering Gypsies in his native land, who supposedly allowed him access to their occult knowledge. Basically, he was a mystic and a magus who left a superb legacy as a palmist. He was one of the first to recognize that some ailments can be detected in the hand, and he wrote a short treatise on this before he died in 1541.

Rudolph Goclenius (1572–1621), a follower of Paracelsus from Wittenberg in Germany, also experimented with palmistry and evidence suggests that he wrote prolifically on the subject.

His first publication appeared while he was still in his teens. Recent studies by scholars, however, have suggested that most of Goclenius' work was actually that of his teacher, Paracelsus. So perhaps the best that can be said of Rudolph Goclenius is that he was among the most talented of the early plagiarists in the field!

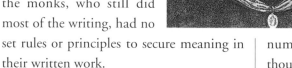

RIGHT Paracelsus, shown in this late 17th-century engraving, was an early proponent of palmistry. He was also a famous astrologer and healer.

RIGHT The Church was deeply suspicious of palmistry and remained an opponent to hand readers in Europe over the centuries.

EARLY WRITINGS ON PALMISTRY

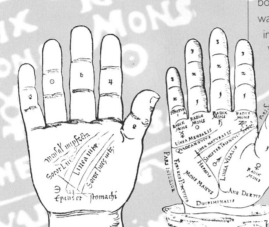

The oldest known palmistry work in English is a manuscript known as the *Digby Roll IV*, dated *circa* 1440. It is in the form of a few strips of vellum about nine inches (22 centimeters) high and some eight inches (20 centimeters) wide, which, when sewn together in the style of the time, formed a strip 87 inches (218 centimeters) long. A copy of the manuscript was published in England in 1953, showing the original writing on one page with the modern literal translation on the facing page. Some fairly basic illustrations were also included.

Two other early English manuscripts exist; they were both written by a John Metham, a scholar from Norfolk, in the 19th century. He claimed to have translated them from the Latin writing of a Doctor Aurelyan, who we know wrote two short works on palmistry. These English translations were published in 1916 by the Early English Text Society.

Other written works on palmistry began appearing elsewhere later in the century. In Germany *Die Kunst Ciromantia*, by Johann Hartlieb, was published in 1475, some six years or so after Hartlieb's death. In 1477 a palmistry book by a Michael Scott called *Die Phisiognomia* was published. A similar book, that was written in both Italian and Latin, was published in Venice in 1480.

In the 16th century John Indagine, a prior from Lower Saxony who had been educated in some of Germany's most exclusive courts, made a substantial contribution with his *Introductiones Apotelesmaticae*. Much that Indagine wrote is incorporated in many early 20th-century publications, and modified versions of some of his original observations on the hand are still in use today. Indagine, though a Catholic priest, also sympathized with Protestant thought and doctrine. In addition, he was a friend to many well-known astrologers of the day. It is not surprising that the text of *Introductiones Apotelesmaticae* was forbidden by the Church when it was first published.

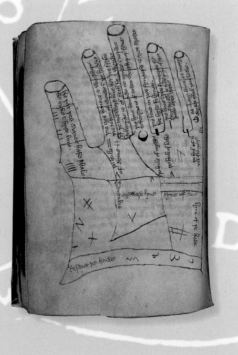

LEFT Early palmistry texts were accompanied with line drawings outlining the shape of the hand marked with signs of the zodiac.

LEFT This manuscript illustration from 1417 confirms a surge of interest in palmistry in medieval Europe.

The Spread of Palmistry

* * * * * * * * * * * * * * * * *

RIGHT The English Cabalist, Robert Fludd (1574–1637), is shown in this portrait surrounded by occult and esoteric symbols associated with his research and writing.

WHILE PALMISTRY continued to develop in Europe during the 16th and 17th centuries, very little seemed to be happening in England. We do know that the Cabalist Robert Fludd (1574–1637) was active in England during this period, because some of his work on hand reading was published in 1661 at Jena in Germany in a collection of writings on palmistry by various authors called *Ludicrum Chiromanticum*. Whatever else may have happened must have occurred in secret. Many still regarded palmistry as the work of the devil, and it was associated with Gypsies, a people who were never fully accepted or trusted in Europe.

Gypsies first appeared in England in the 14th century, but by 1530 they had earned such a terrible reputation for theft and criminal activity that Henry VIII issued a statute which condemned to death any Gypsy who was caught on the wrong side of the law. No one knew exactly where the Gypsies had come from, or where they had learned the art of palmistry. Many thought that they were originally from Egypt – hence their name. Others, however, believed that these "Egyptians" were actually from India, where the art of palmistry was a well-known and highly respected practice by people of all variety of social ranks.

RIGHT A Gypsy fortune teller reads the palm of a nobleman. The art of palmistry was widely practiced by the Gypsies in Europe from the Middle Ages onward.

It is an old belief that it was the Gypsies who introduced palmistry to Britain, but early documentation disproves this myth. Nevertheless, their persecution by Henry VIII undoubtedly fueled this belief, and there is still distrust of Gypsies in many rural areas of Britain today.

By the mid-17th century, palmistry once more began to emerge from the darkness in England. In 1652 George Wharton, a man already well known for publishing almanacs, published a translation of the work of a famous continental palmist and author named Rothmann. The following year one of Wharton's compatriots, Richard Saunders (1613–1683?), wrote his first palmistry works *Physiognomie* and *Chiromancie, Metoscopie*. These were milestones in English publishing.

Saunders was a friend of the astrologer William Lilly, and astrology was really his first love. But his publications on palmistry revolutionized the field in their time.

Saunders' first work, while largely original and the result of his own research, also included highly suspect wholesale copying of work by the French palmist Jean Belot. Saunders did acknowledge some of this. But in 1664 he produced a second work, *Palmistry, the Secrets Disclosed,* in which Belot is not acknowledged. However, Saunders' remarkably accurate personality and character interpretations, based on the chirognomy of the hand, do seem to come from earlier sources, which would suggest that his findings may not have been

his alone. Nonetheless, the book is still viewed with respect today and is well worth reading – it is invaluable for the way it reflects the thinking of the time.

Generally speaking, the 18th century was a rather quiet time for almost all occult studies. Only one man, the Swiss Johann Kaspar Lavater (1741–1801), stands out: a pious and devout Protestant minister, Lavater was also a poet and the author of several books on physiognomy held to be landmarks in their field and much prized today. Though he seems to have had only slight knowledge of palmistry, he made references to hands in all his books, and his work helped to keep palmistry alive until the next century.

A Woman's Realm

★ ★ ★ ★ ★ ★ ★ ★ ★ ★ ★ ★ ★ ★ ★

THE FIRST women palmists arrived on the scene in the 19th century. Marie-Anne le Normand, born in France in September 1768, was a seer who could read Tarot cards with great proficiency. She claimed her powers were of Egyptian origin because in those days Egyptology was all the rage. Through sheer chance, she met the Emperor Napoleon and made some predictions for him, some of which were based on a reading of his hands. What she foretold worried Napoleon; in fact, he feared her "gifts" so much that he had her arrested and detained in December 1809 until his divorce became final.

As a palmist, le Normand was a pure charlatan. If necessary, she would break every rule in the book in order to "prove" a point or validate a prediction. Her book, *Souvenirs*

Prophétiques, gives us an indication of her feverish and overactive imagination. That, and her complete lack of knowledge concerning palmar geography, reveal how much damage people like her can do if given too much rein.

The second woman to stand out in the history of palmistry, Adële Moreau, was also French and in fact was a disciple of le Normand. Moreau was almost as bad as her teacher. In 1869 she produced her book, *Chiromancie Nouvelle.* It is a marvelous book on the social history of the times, despite being wildly inaccurate in places and totally misleading in others. Still, it does have a few saving graces – photography is used for the first time in a palmistry book and shows that Moreau knew how to use handprints.

The next woman to appear on the palmistry scene was an Australian who settled in England; her name was Katherine St. Hill. One of the founders in 1889 of the English Chirological Society, she had a completely different approach to any of her predecessors. Unlike le Normand and Moreau, St. Hill was methodical, very persistent, and nearly always got her way. Doors opened to her as they never had to anyone else. She was allowed into prisons, hospitals, and mental asylums, and given almost total freedom to do her research. In her many books, all of them classics of their time, she has given posterity much valuable data not only on palmistry but also on Victorian society in England.

RIGHT Katherine St. Hill's pioneering approach to palmistry has left us with a great legacy of detailed research and writings on the subject.

RIGHT *The Reader of Hands,* as this 19th-century painting is entitled, intrigues her audience as she reveals the meaning of her subject's palm.

Ina Oxenford, who was treasurer of the Chirological Society, wrote marvelous books with well-founded ideas that have stood the test of time. There were also many others in the group, both men and women, who published their findings. Unfortunately, however, the Society began to waver in its dedication and eventually lost its way. It closed down just prior to the turn of the century, although a dedicated handful of its members continued with some experiments.

Shortly after the start of the 20th century one man began to dominate the palmistry scene: Count Louis Hamon, also known as Cheiro, was perhaps the most successful palmist ever. He read hands brilliantly and he wrote many books that became landmarks of palmistry. He had the gift of seership and was a clever numerologist with a good working knowledge of astrology.

Born in Dublin on November 1, 1886, Cheiro was an egomaniac with an extremely inventive imagination. It is probably better to remember his achievements in hand analysis rather than the other adventures, for although his own accounts of his life are dramatic, colorful, and highly entertaining, they are perhaps not entirely truthful.

We do know, however, that Cheiro was one of the first of the modern supersalesmen. He was able to sell just about anything to anyone, including himself – it is evident that he honestly believed that some of his stories were actually true. But while his claims of travels in the East and his study of ancient writings may be lively and convincing, almost everything he wrote can be traced back to Chirological Society sources.

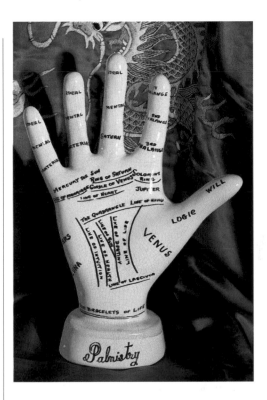

Cheiro's first book, *The Language of the Hand*, published when he was still in his twenties, was brilliant and made him famous. In some cases stars may be forgiven for some of their excesses, and Cheiro certainly belongs to this group. His services to palmistry far outweigh any of his exaggerations or fabrications.

The turn of the century also saw a surge of interest in hand reading in America, a development helped immeasurably by William Benham, the first and probably still the best American palmist. Benham's classic text, *The Laws of Scientific Hand Reading*, was published in 1900 to instant success. Often called the palmists' bible, it is over 600 pages long and crammed with facts. It does not preach, but allows the reader to make up his or her own mind. It is a must for any aspiring student of hand reading.

A Modern Approach to Palmistry

* * * * * * * * * * * * * * * * * *

THROUGHOUT THE 20TH century palmistry has continued to grow, develop, and spread across the world, with findings now being freely shared by researchers and practitioners. For those who wish to take their studies further, there is abundant documentation on the more recent developments in modern palmistry.

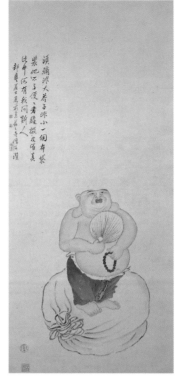

One major development is the study of dermatoglyphics, the capillary-line skin patterns on the surface of the fingers and the palm. Centuries ago, the Chinese knew that these hand markings were unique. Their emperors used thumbprints to seal letters of state, and many other kinds of documents and legal papers were "signed" or sealed with an individual's thumbprint. This practice was also common in Egypt, India, Japan, and other parts of the world.

In the early 19th century in Bohemia (now known as the Czech Republic), Johann Evangelista Purkinje (1787–1869) gained a qualification in medicine and became a professor of anatomy and physiology at Breslau. In 1823 he published his paper on fingerprint patterns and in it referred to the palmar skin patterns as well. He discussed the possible use of fingerprints for identification and classified their diverse patterns as far as he was able. This marks the birth of modern dermatoglyphics.

In 1892 Francis Galton discovered Purkinje's papers and referred to them in his book on the fingerprint system. William Herschel, Alphonse Bertillon, Henry Faulds, and Edward Henry – major contributors to the development and research into finger- and palm-print patterns – all acknowledged the value of Purkinje's original work.

Out of Purkinje's work, and that of those who followed, has come the most modern approach to palmistry. This work has followed a twofold path: one in criminal identification and crime detection; the other in palmistry, where interpreting the loops and swirls of these patterns helps in character and personality assessment.

Since the early 20th century hospitals and research centers all over the world have been using dermatoglyphics to conduct tests and trials in many areas of medical research and every so often some of their findings are published. By contrast, it is quite rare to hear of developments in palmistry techniques that use skin patterns.

One fairly recent progression in palmistry is the study and use of hand and body gesture, popularly known as "body

RIGHT In ancient China, documents were sealed with thumbprints, which the Chinese understood to be unique to the individual.

BELOW Francis Galton, shown in this painting by Charles Wellington Furse, discovered Purkinje's papers which he found invaluable in his own study of dermatology.

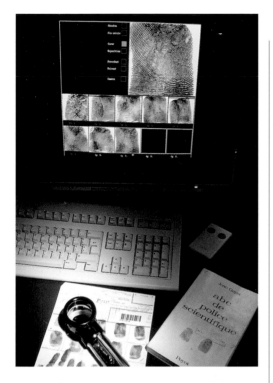

language." Many hand analysts now use this relatively new behavioral science, which has already proven to be a virtually inexhaustible supply of information.

We tend to show our true nature by our actions, speech, and gestures, and whether or not we are aware of it, we all use our hands in conversation and communication with others. Nor is gesture confined to the hands. We also communicate with our bodies. People make tiny movements when talking to others, which can be classified in four basic categories: nervous, emotional, intellectual, and social.

Hand analysts who study body language will observe every move their clients make – how they walk, how they shake hands (or if they don't shake hands!), how they sit, and what gestures they make during the consultation. This is not too different from doctors who often do the same thing during

a medical checkup. Certain gestures are known to suggest certain illnesses or physical conditions, and a good doctor will look for them when making a diagnosis.

This new four-way approach to character and personality assessment – chiromancy, chirognomy, dermatoglyphics, and body language – is a far cry from the image of the Gypsy fortune teller who spoke of tall, dark strangers and voyages across the water. A modern palmist can offer guidance, advice, and help in many different areas of life. He or she can help people uncertain of their direction in life find their proper niche by showing them where their real talents, abilities, and aptitudes lie. People dissatisfied with their jobs can be directed toward work that might be more suited to their needs and abilities. And, since palmistry deals with character and personality, it can be a valuable tool in solving some of the difficulties that may arise in close personal relationships.

From a past cloaked in mystery, through periods of adversity, opposition, and even persecution, palmistry has nonetheless stood the test of time. By remaining open to change, it has grown and developed, and continues to do so today.

LEFT Advances in technology have enabled modern-day hand analysts to process and catalog finger and thumb-prints taken from individuals all over the world.

LEFT A scientist is wearing red-filtered glasses to protect his eyes from a laser that is able to detect the fingerprints left on this gun.

HANDPRINTS

* * * * * * * * * * * * * * * * * *

HANDPRINTS ARE AN essential part of hand analysis, for they provide permanent records for the palmist. Interviews are all very well, but one can never be expected to remember every physical feature of the hand afterward. It makes sense to record the hands you read to provide a reference for the future.

As you build your collection of handprints into a library, they will provide valuable source material to which you may constantly refer. For example, themes can emerge when dealing with members of the same family. You may find patterns in members of the same profession, or in people with similar medical conditions, which may furnish useful information later on. No matter how often you look at a set of handprints, you can always find something of interest that you missed before.

Therapeutic work is aided by continuous record making. Many different themes run through the life of any individual, and prints taken at regular intervals help show the changes we all experience in our lives. Being able to refer to these prints not only helps the analyst, but is also of great value to the subject. Furthermore, should your subject come back later for another interview, you will have a ready-made record to which you may refer should you need to do so.

To make handprints you will need a small sheet of plate-glass about 12 inches (30 centimeters) square (round will also do); a 4-inch (10-centimeter) photographer's roller; an 8- by 11-inch (or European A4) sheet of white paper; a wooden rolling pin about 2 inches (5–6 centimeters) in diameter; and a tube of black water-based printing ink.

Fingerprint ink may be used, but it is very difficult to remove from the hands and equipment afterward. Water-based ink simply flows off when the hands are held under cold, running water for a few moments. Afterward, the hands may be washed in warm, soapy water. It is essential to use cold water for the first rinse. Rinsing first in warm or hot water will open the pores and cause the ink to get ingrained, making it much more difficult to remove.

Taking handprints can be frustrating at first, but the procedure becomes easier with practice, and you will soon be able to make expert prints every time.

Start by squeezing about 1 inch (2–3 centimeters) of ink onto the glass. Roll it out until you achieve an even consistency, with no little bubbles, bumps, or other marks. The ink on the roller should be fairly thin – the thicker the ink, the more likely it is to obscure some of the lines on the palm.

The hand to be inked should be as clean as possible; grease or dirt can blur the image. It will also help if any jewelry is removed. (Do remember, however, that some people prefer not to take off their wedding ring.)

Ink the hand by rolling in one direction only. Cover the outer edges of the palm and fingers evenly, and try to include up to 3 inches (6–7 centimeters) of the wrist area.

At the far side of the table, put a sheet of paper on the rolling pin. Have the subject place his or her wrist near the bottom edge of the paper and roll the hand back over the rolling pin. While your subject is doing this, try to make sure the pressure is even and that the thumb and fingertips print out. At the end of the roll, lift the hand cleanly away from the paper, and you should have a perfect print. Always take the hand from the print, not the paper from the hand.

Thumbprints should be taken separately. Keeping the paper at the near edge of the table, place the thumb on the bottom edge of the paper. Roll the thumb gently in one direction only, or you will smudge the result.

If there is a problem with the rolling-pin method, put a folded dishtowel under the paper and place the subject's hand squarely on top of the paper and the towel. Press gently in the middle of the palm and at the fingertips. Holding the paper at the corners, have your subject lift the hand swiftly upward. If in turn this does not work, try the slap method. Ink the hand as before, place

BELOW Handprints are invaluable as a record of the individual's hand. You will need the following equipment to make a print:

a square sheet of plate glass

a tube of water-based ink

a magnifying glass

a wooden rolling-pin

a sheet of 8- x 11- inch (A4) paper

a 4-inch (10cm) photographer's roller

MAKING PRINTS

1 Squeeze about an inch (3cm) of ink onto the sheet glass and, using a photographer's roller, spread it out evenly.

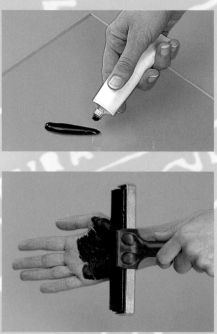

2 Ink the subject's clean hand using the roller. Remember to roll it one direction at a time.

3 Roll the subject's hand over the A4 sheet of white paper resting on the rolling pin.

4 Alternatively, put a folded dishtowel under the paper and ask the subject to slap their inked hand firmly down onto the paper before lifting it straight up again.

the paper on the towel, and have the subject hold the hand about six or eight inches (15–20 centimeters) above the paper. He or she should then slap the paper quickly and firmly, straight down and up again.

Handprints can be taken even from people with serious hand infirmities, although the degree of incapacity will obviously affect the legibility of the print. Ink the subject's hand as described, then place the paper on the upturned hand. Using another, dry, roller, make the print in reverse.

It should be possible to take three or four copies of the palmar surface before having to ink the hand once again. (Gently breathing on the inked hand will moisten the ink a little.) The finished print should dry in about four or five minutes.

If for any reason you prefer not to use ink, you can use lipstick, or indeed any other available marking medium, instead. With a few practice runs, you can even make readable handprints on an ordinary flatbed photocopier. When using a photocopier, cover the back of the hand with a cloth to block out any extraneous light. Adjust the copier's light/dark setting as necessary.

Whatever method you use, always clearly mark each print "LEFT" or "RIGHT." Some photocopiers produce a reverse image, so it is easy to get confused later on.

One final idea, not for copying but for immediate close examination of hand markings, is to dust the palms very lightly with talcum powder and then gently rub the hands together. All the features on the palm should be thrown into relief, making a reading of the hand much easier.

BUILDING A LIBRARY OF HANDPRINTS

LEFT A computer system will help you to establish a library of handprint data and will save hours as your collection of prints increases.

Building a library of handprints is not difficult and can be great fun. On the reverse of the handprint, or on a separate record card (to keep the chances of damaging the print to a minimum), write a description of the rest of the hand. Include the following details:

• General description of the back of the hand.

• Color and skin texture.

• Nail descriptions.

• Flexibility of the hand and fingers.

• Knots and knuckles.

• Any special features or peculiarities.

RIGHT You can record relevant information on the reverse of your prints or set up your own card system.

Use a simple filing system to build your library – perhaps arranging the prints alphabetically by subject's name. If you have a computer, so much the better; it will make cross-referencing data quick and easy. The enormous speed with which these machines can process information will save hours as your library increases.

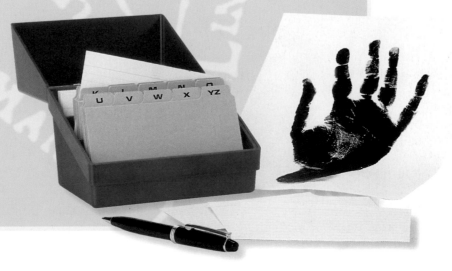

PART ONE

THE SHAPE OF THE HAND

★ ★ ★ ★ ★

Think of the hand as new and undiscovered country ready for you to explore. It has a unique shape – an outline – and within this outline are valleys, forests, rivers, roads, villages, towns, and cities. To find your way through this newfound country you will need a map. And in order to read the map effectively you will need to bear in mind the basic elements of the terrain over which you intend to make your journey.

ABOVE The shape of the hand informs the palmist during the interpretation of the main lines and other features.

For example, a road crossing a plain will allow you to see more of what is going on than a road that passes through a forest. A river has one personality when it is relatively still, and a completely different one when it suddenly drops and turns into a waterfall. A city may be large or small in relation to its surroundings.

Similarly, in palmistry, lines tend to retain their basic meaning from hand to hand, but take on slightly different interpretations according to the type of hand on which they appear. The shape of the hand will alter the meaning of the main palmar lines, and other minor features or marks will take on meanings according to the hand on which they are found.

TRADITIONAL CLASSIFICATION

* * * * * * * * * * * * * * * * *

TRADITIONALLY THERE ARE seven basic hand shapes, although some modern chirologists suggest that there are just four. Essentially there are only two actual shapes: the square, rectangular, or "useful" hand; and the round or conic, often called the "artistic" hand. All other hand shapes are variations on these two basic themes.

Before starting a reading, it is important to assess the basic hand shape, so first decide if it appears either square or round. Always make your decision based on a frontal, or palmar, view. A hand can appear to be one shape when viewed from the front and can look entirely different when it is turned over, and many hands look more square when viewed from the back. If the general appearance of the front of the hand is square or rectangular, then that is the hand's basic shape.

BELOW People with square hands tend to have practical qualities – they are doers rather than thinkers.

THE SQUARE HAND

The edges of the square hand seem straight, and so does the base of the hand across the wrist. The set of the fingers may be arched, sloping, or even, or the index (first) and fourth fingers can be equally lower set. The fingers themselves can be long or short, thick or thin, straight or crooked. Regardless of these variations, the whole hand, including the fingers, should look square in

order to be classified as such. Generally, square palms tend to have fewer lines than palms on conic hands.

People with a square or "useful" hand tend to be conventional, a little set in their ways, with great respect for law and order. These are the folks who are able to do all those little practical jobs many others cannot do. They are orderly, logical, methodical, and levelheaded and often demonstrate endless patience. They are determined, sometimes to the point of stubbornness. Almost anything new and untried is viewed with great suspicion. Square-handed people rarely show affection in public, although they feel things very deeply.

THE ROUND OR CONIC HAND

In palmistry, "conic" is an old term for round. When the hand and fingers appear conic there is a slight tapering to the fingertips, and the edges of the hand seem soft in comparison to a square hand. The ulna, or outer edge of the palm, usually has a definite curve or bulge to it.

People with this hand shape tend to be creative and artistic. A conic hand implies impulse and idealism, the sort of person who makes and breaks relationships with equal ease, not through lack of feeling but because of a continuing need for new and different experiences. These are people who have to keep on the move, who have a low boredom threshold and are at their most destructive when they have nothing to do. They care little for the old ways of doing things – it is the new and modern that stimulates them, and they will try anything once.

BELOW Those who possess a square hand are practical, rational, and persevering.

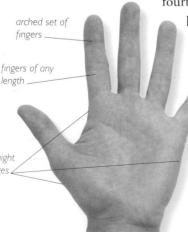

arched set of fingers

fingers of any length

straight edges

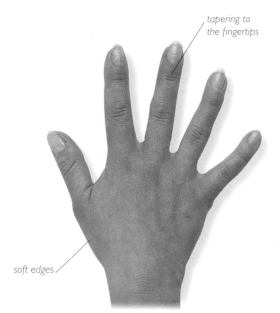

tapering to the fingertips

soft edges

A round hand suggests a Jack or Jill of all trades, but one whose knowledge is superficial. He or she can talk easily, and at times very convincingly, on many subjects, but without genuine depth of knowledge. The life of the party, often the first on the dance floor, such people may have an inherent lazy streak and perhaps a little selfishness. Moody, imaginative, they recover from setbacks with great ease, full of their usual charm and magnetism again.

THE ELEMENTARY HAND

This type of hand looks short and clumsy, with a thick, heavy palm, stubby fingers, and badly kept nails. The thumb is fairly thick from the bottom upwards, and sometimes looks as if it is an afterthought.

This shape suggests an uncomplicated personality, someone slow to perceive and act, and this is largely accurate. But if this person's thinking is slow, it is more instinctive. These people know enough to stay away from anything they do not understand, and this can sometimes lead others to misunderstand them. However, they should not be considered fools. They are gifted with a good feel for and knowledge of nature, which gives them an instinctive approach to all sorts of problems.

If the fingers on an elementary palm appear noticeably long, which tends to happen frequently, the owner is likely to have good basic skills in a recognized trade or craft. People with an elementary hand may lack imagination and subtlety, but they almost always make up for this with a sound, commonsensical approach to just about everything that they choose to do. They know what is right and wrong and are basically honest.

LEFT People with conic hands are impulsive, sensitive, and full of charm.

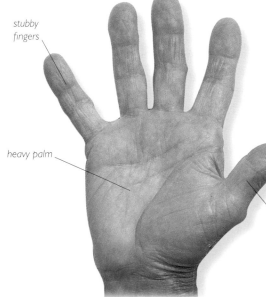

ABOVE A carpenter at work. It is people with elementary hands who tend to have skills in a recognized trade.

LEFT Down-to-earth, those with elementary hands nearly always use common sense.

stubby fingers

heavy palm

Thick thumb from the base upward.

THE PSYCHIC HAND

This shape is an extreme version of the round or conic type, with a long palm and slender fingers that taper to a point. These hands are always beautifully kept, often with immaculate, almond-shaped nails. The whole hand has a soft, genteel appearance.

Owners of this hand live lives of such total mental and emotional idealism that they are not suited to the cut and thrust of the modern world. Far from practical, they have little or no business sense and can be excessively trusting. They will confide in all the wrong people and usually end up deeply hurt as a result. Unfortunately, they tend not to learn from their mistakes. Such idealistic and visionary types should stay far away from the harsh realities of the everyday world.

People whose psychic hand has a strong thumb and/or a firm palm are well suited to positions of authority requiring diplomacy. Often, these people may display gifts in areas where culture, taste, and discernment are of prime importance such as food and wine or jewelry, and are fastidious where health and hygiene matters are concerned.

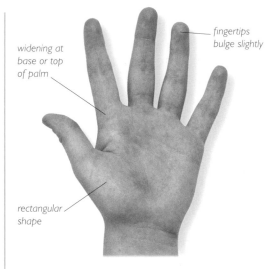

widening at
base or top
of palm

fingertips
bulge slightly

rectangular
shape

THE SPATULATE HAND

This is largely a variation on the basic square hand type. The spatulate hand is rarely an extension of the round shape, but has been known to happen occasionally.

Generally speaking, this hand looks more rectangular than square and has a clearly defined widening either at the base of the hand near the wrist, or at the top of the hand where the fingers begin. Often, but not always, the tips of the fingers have a spatulate appearance and seem to bulge slightly.

Basically these folks are extremely restless – highly strung and full of energy. Rarely satisfied, they always want more. They are unconventional and even eccentric at times. Strongly independent, they are also highly inventive, which may be expressed as a natural talent for innovation or simply a desire to change the world. They can be ingenious, and will often tinker with things or look for ways to improve old, established routines. Given time, they may come up with entirely new ways of doing things, often more economical than existing methods.

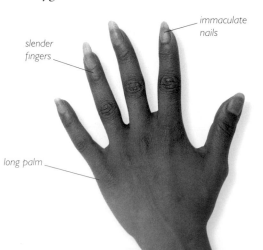

immaculate
nails

slender
fingers

long palm

THE PHILOSOPHIC HAND

Essentially this is a long, bony, square or rectangular hand. The palm seems quite cramped or even narrow; the fingers are distinguished by clearly defined knuckles and noticeable bulges at each joint.

These people think and feel emotions very deeply. As lone wolves, they tend to be left to their own devices, especially since few people seem to understand them. Even fewer people can cope with them, and fewer still can live with them. It really does take the patience of a saint and the wisdom of Solomon to partner this type.

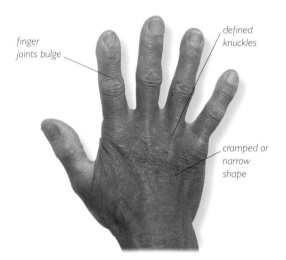

finger joints bulge

defined knuckles

cramped or narrow shape

However, philosophic types are not wholly antisocial – far from it – when they turn on their charm they can be refined, cultured, shrewd, and entertaining. They display good manners and have a perceptive and often mischievous or impish sense of humor. Dignified and proud, they have a "presence" that is always noted. They may often be found among leaders in education, religion, science, psychology, or psychiatry.

THE MIXED HAND

Mixed hands can be confusing, for they do not conform to any of the usual groups and can easily be mistaken for an extreme version of any of the other six types.

Some mixed hands may seem to be just like the psychic hand, others may be partly spatulate at the top or bottom of the palm but after a close check will actually turn out to be square. The fingers may all be different; the golden rule is to observe. If the hand does not comply with all the usual requirements then you must accept the hand for what it is – mixed.

People with this type of hand are adaptable. Versatile and changeable, they are always on the lookout for anything new. They can also be inconsistent and quite volatile. For them, challenge is the accepted norm, and they are always prepared to take a chance and try anything once – twice if they like it. Red tape and the petty bureaucratic life are not for them. There is a strong selfish streak – mixed-hand people look out for themselves, often to the exclusion of others.

LEFT Deeply emotional, philosophic types may seem withdrawn but in fact they are good company and possess great leadership skills.

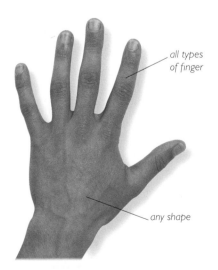

all types of finger

any shape

LEFT Flexibility is characteristic of the mixed hand – but beware their selfish streak!

MODERN CLASSIFICATION

* * * * * * * * * * * * * * * *

THIS IS ANOTHER way of classifying hand shapes that follows the principles of the four elements: Fire, Earth, Air, and Water. A largely modern innovation, there is a lot to be said for this slightly easier way of categorizing hand shapes, but it is rather simplistic, because it tries to condense many features into only four shapes. This usually works, but my own personal view is that this classification allows for no variations within the hand. When it doesn't work, and a hand does not appear to belong to any of the new categories, it will almost certainly be easier to assign it to one of the older, more traditional classifications.

ABOVE The fire hand, according to traditional classification, has a long palm topped by short fingers.

CENTER The identification of a Fire, Earth, Air, or Water hand is a modern method of classifying hand shapes.

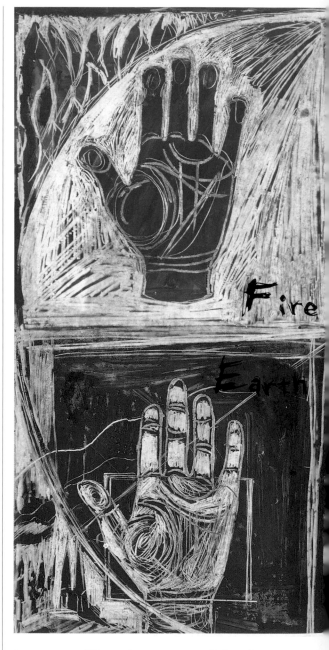

Fire

Earth

THE FIRE HAND

The Fire hand comprises a long palm topped by fingers shorter than the palm. The fingers may be slightly wider at their tips – not quite spatulate, but almost.

People with this hand shape are outgoing, dynamic, vital, and enthusiastic. Rarely still for long, they have to have something to do, to keep their hands and mind occupied. They are usually fond of sports or outdoor pursuits and are the life and soul of any gathering. Leaders rather than followers, they take charge naturally, almost as a matter of course. They have to monitor their energy reserves or they are liable to burn themselves out.

THE EARTH HAND

This type of hand has square palms with fingers slightly shorter than the palm. Almost without exception, these people tend to be solid and down-to-earth, with few

ABOVE The Earth hand, which belongs to practical nature lovers, is square with short fingers.

hang-ups. They have a traditional, conventional outlook and respect law and order. There is often a very strong creative side to their nature, but their creativity is practical and probably linked somehow with manual dexterity. They love the outdoors,

THE AIR HAND

The Air hand is a square hand shape, but with fingers longer than the palm and often quite supple and flexible.

Mental pursuits of all kinds appeal to these people. Good at languages and communication in general, they are brilliant when it comes to modern technology such as computers. They have a constant need to be kept busy and thrive on tight deadlines and strict timetables. If they sit around for too long, their restless streak may work against them and get them into trouble. Travel attracts them because it exposes them to ever-changing scenery.

These people control their emotional responses by approaching problems with logic rather than allowing their feelings to surface for others to see. But by applying the brakes like this, they not only avoid some of life's pain, they also miss out on much of its joy and happiness.

ABOVE Those with a head for technology will probably have an Air hand – square palms with long, flexible fingers.

THE WATER HAND

These hands have long palms with long fingers. Their owners are very emotionally responsive, and highly sensitive to changes of mood, color, or atmosphere.

Most people with this hand shape are creative and attracted to the arts. They are not materialists, and may spend their lives working or caring for others. Because they get so caught up with things, they have to learn to keep both feet very firmly on the ground. A new romance, for instance, can send them soaring into a world of their own. They tend to be vulnerable to bullies and other insensitive types.

ABOVE The Water hand is long and denotes the sensitive, creative type. These types are vulnerable.

are close to nature, and often have a great love of animals. They are dependable friends, loyal and honest not only with others, but with themselves as well. However, they can become a little impatient when things do not go quite as planned.

TRADITIONAL PALMISTRY: THE MOUNTS

★ ★ ★ ★ ★ ★ ★ ★ ★ ★ ★ ★ ★ ★ ★ ★ ★

TRADITIONAL HAND READING, or palmistry, divides the hand into areas called mounts, while modern hand analysis, or chirology, places more emphasis on areas of the palm known as zones. It is valuable to look at both methods, since using a combination of both can give highly accurate readings.

ABOVE An Elizabethan illustration depicting different zones on the palm.

ABOVE The god Saturn is depicted in this 16th-century manuscript. The Saturn mount is said to regulate balance in character.

the Jupiter mount

THE JUPITER MOUNT
Set under the first or Jupiter finger, this mount is associated with qualities such as pride, integrity, ambition, and religious and spiritual leanings. People with a normally developed Jupiter mount will have a good social sense, a certain charm of manner, and built-in leadership qualities. Others instinctively trust them and tend to follow their lead whenever possible.

When this mount is overdeveloped, expect to find selfishness and a bossy, overbearing nature coupled with arrogance, narrow-mindedness and bigotry. The person with an underdeveloped Jupiter mount is usually a somewhat lazy person, with little ambition and a strong dislike of authority.

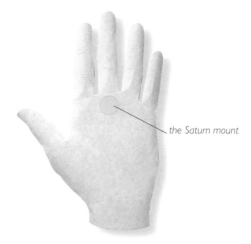

the Saturn mount

THE SATURN MOUNT
Located beneath the middle finger, also known as the finger of balance, this mount is said to regulate the stability of one's character. If it is too well developed, however, the owner is likely to have a gloomy, cynical, or unforgiving attitude to life. This person is usually somewhat cautious and may be a trifle more sensitive to the outside world than average.

Those with an underdeveloped Saturn mount lack not only a sense of humor, but also a sense of responsibility. In some cases they may be superstitious as well. A moderate development of this mount allows for a plain, commonsense approach to life.

THE APOLLO MOUNT
Found under the third finger, this mount reflects creative talents, artistic appreciation, and sociability. People with a normal development here have bright and cheerful dispositions. When this mount is overdeveloped, however, expect to find a misplaced sense of sentimentality, along with

the Apollo mount

some ostentation, narcissism, and over-assertiveness. An underdeveloped mount implies a lack of refinement, a poor or dull personality with few if any esthetic values.

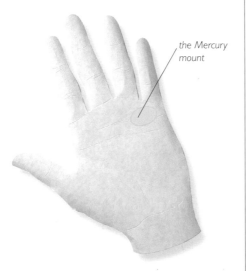

the Mercury mount

THE MERCURY MOUNT

This mount represents our overall ability to communicate; it should lean slightly toward the Apollo mount rather than sit directly under the fourth finger. If the mount is normally developed, the owner will display a ready wit and a talent for commercial life.

If overdeveloped, he will be prone to taking chances without planning properly. Although not deliberately dishonest, these people may not always be entirely truthful with themselves or others. A flat mount indicates poor personal expression.

THE VENUS MOUNT

Strictly speaking, this is not a mount but the third phalange of the thumb. It reflects our physical energy and well-being, and the level of the libido. Those with a normally developed mount have excellent stamina and vitality, while those with an overdeveloped mount generally have a more than healthy sex drive and a real zest for life.

A full, healthy-looking mount suggests a contented personality. These people run their home well and keep the welcome mat out for anyone at any time. They like other people and have good social and family relationships. An underdeveloped, flat, or lifeless mount, however, indicates a somewhat cold nature. Such people are often selfish in their relationships, and any unexpected visitors can expect a cool reception at best. As a general rule, they do not even get along with members of their own family.

Always look at both hands when assessing this mount, because there is often a marked difference between them. This can account for mood swings or changeable behavior in the subject.

ABOVE Venus, the goddess of love, is shown here holding the romantic symbols of a mirror and a flower. The mount of Venus denotes our physical energy and libido.

ABOVE This Roman statue depicts the god Apollo. In palmistry, the Apollo mount relates to artistic talent and creativity.

the Venus mount

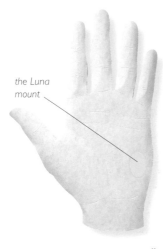

the Luna mount

ABOVE If the Luna mount is healthy expect to find a sense of caring.

THE LUNA MOUNT

Also known as the mount of the Moon, this is the padded area extending from halfway down the outer edge of the hand to the base of the palm. It indicates our imaginative, subconscious and intuitive powers – our "sensitivity" to life.

When this mount is normally developed expect to find an artistic approach to life. A well-developed mount shows a strong sense of caring, a love of peace and harmony, and a desire to please and be pleased. The owner may also have a practical creative talent.

A poorly developed, flat, lifeless mount suggests a somewhat dull personality. There is a lack of "sparkle" and the owner may be hesitant, with very little imagination.

ABOVE Luna, god of the planets, is drawn across the heavens in a chariot. The Luna mount indicates our "sensitivity" to life.

A Luna mount that encroaches on the Venus mount is a sign of an intensely passionate or emotional nature. However, when the Venus mount moves toward the Luna mount, it implies poorly channeled excess physical energy.

THE NEPTUNE MOUNT

This mount is set at the base of the palm between the Venus mount and the Luna mount. Because of its position, it can be considered as either a link between the unconscious and conscious sides of the palm or as a barrier or obstacle between them.

TOP CENTER The sea god Neptune rears above the waves – those with a Neptune mount are fun-loving and sociable.

When this mount is present, it suggests a lively character, someone who understands people and is fun to be with. If the mount is overdeveloped, these qualities will be accentuated. But if the mount is flat or nonexistent, the person is considerably less sociable and may even dislike people.

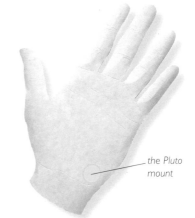

the Pluto mount

THE PLUTO MOUNT

As with the Neptune mount, treating this bottom section of the Luna pad as a mount in its own right is a relatively modern concept in palmistry. When this area is well developed the owner generally has an interest, either practical or only theoretical, in the occult and all matters supernatural. If the mount is poorly developed, he or she probably has a skeptical attitude toward subjects such as astrology or the occult.

the Neptune mount

THE ZONE OF MARS

The center of the palm reflects the way we interact with our immediate environment. The zone of Mars incorporates the traditional Upper, Lower and Plain of Mars.

Upper Mars is tucked between the thumb and the base of the Jupiter mount. When this is normally developed there will be plenty of physical courage, with sufficient energy to support it. If overdeveloped this will be accentuated, but if underdeveloped there may be a bullying or cowardly nature.

Lower Mars, between the base of the Mercury mount and the top of the Luna mount, indicates the strength of the owner's integrity and moral convictions. Most people have some development here, but if it is flat, expect to find poor staying power and an inability to cope under pressure.

the Mars mounts

Upper Mars (Mars positive)

Plain of Mars

Lower Mars (Mars negative)

The Plain of Mars lies between these two outer areas. The only way to test it is by touch rather than sight alone. If the area feels spongy and fleshy, then it is developed. If it feels bony and thin, then it is underdeveloped, regardless of what it may actually look like. When it feels well developed, there is almost always an interest in worldly affairs, possibly an active one which translates into a definite role – politician or government official. An underdeveloped area shows little interest in any international matters.

the Creative Curve

THE CREATIVE CURVE

This is not really a mount but the curve down the outer edge of the hand from the base of the little finger to the wrist. It can extend the whole way or only part of it. The more obvious the curve the greater the subject's creative energy; the straighter the edge the less this will be apparent.

The curve, if pronounced at the top of the hand, suggests good mental creativity but little practical ability to carry out ideas; if toward the middle, skill at realizing concepts. A basal emphasis indicates practicality.

THE HEALTH MOUNT

When the thumb is held close to the hand or clenched into a fist, a small bulge is created at the back of the hand. If firm it denotes good health with strong recuperative powers. A soft mount implies a weaker constitution, someone who is susceptible to bugs and is slow to recover.

When the mounts on both hands are full and firm the subject enjoys company and has a natural zest for life. If the mounts are low and soft the owner tends not to join in, and lacks zeal and purpose.

BELOW Mars, god of war, surges toward battle in his chariot. The palmist looks for the mount of Mars in the center of the palm.

BELOW To check the health mount, rest the thumb on top of the Apollo finger and make a fist.

The health mount – the "mouse" or bulge denotes good health.

MODERN CHIROLOGY: THE AREAS

* * * * * * * * * * * * * * * * * *

*zone of
balance*

*ulna and
instinctive
zone*

*radial and
active zone*

In MODERN HAND analysis the hand is divided first into three longitudinal zones, then into three equal horizontal areas, giving a total of nine distinct sectors. A separate meaning could be assigned to each section, but modern analysts tend to refer to the zones by group.

The first of the longitudinal divisions is the radial zone, which extends from the thumb side of the hand to just beyond the space between the first and second fingers. An imaginary line running down the palm from here would just about take in all of the whole mount of Venus.

The radial or active side of the hand shows how we react to external stimuli. People whose hands have a well-developed radial side must have freedom to act as they see fit; they will resist any sort of restrictions.

A firm, straight, long first finger indicates an observant individual who also enjoys being observed by others. This person takes great pride in what he or she does. If, when the hand is relaxed, this finger remains close to the middle finger, the person is not very adaptable. If this finger is short, or shorter

than the Apollo finger, there will be bad leadership ability and even an inferiority complex.

A good Jupiter mount, with a pronounced mount of Negative Mars, indicates assertiveness and leadership ability. When there is a strong thumb as well, the leadership is practical. If in addition there is a full Venus mount, there is plenty of stamina to fall back on.

The middle area, called the zone of balance, extends to about the middle of the third finger. Extended downward, the line would reach slightly to the outer edge of the center of the base of the palm. When this area is well developed and well balanced, with a strong finger and mount of Saturn at the top, there is a balance between action and instinct. But there is no such balance if this zone is not developed, and the subject will have problems with judgment and decision making.

When there is no fate line (see pages 76–82) to help balance the overall character, there will be a lack of responsibility and self-discipline and little effort will be made to

"ideal world" zone

mental zone

material zone

redress this. Not surprisingly, others find this person unreliable.

The third zone stretches out to the percussion, the instinctive side of the hand. If well developed the owner is clever but deceptive and can often bluff his or her way out of the trickiest situation. Such people can create their own opportunities, often from scanty resources. A full percussion, firm to the touch, and with a creative curve indicates that they will be most likely to succeed through their creative instincts.

If the outer edge of the hand is poorly developed it is hard to know how the subject thinks or acts. These people rarely succeed in business, for they simply haven't got the hard edge needed to get to the top. Social life is also limited, and the person doesn't have much natural *joie de vivre*.

The top horizontal zone, traditionally called the "ideal world," takes in all the fingers down to where they join the palm. When this area is well developed, the subject has the best intentions and good leadership abilities, often only used with adequate support from the middle zone.

A fully developed middle area, or mental zone, suggests good business acumen, shrewdness, and a good eye for a bargain. The subject usually has plenty of physical energy and stamina to back up these abilities. Worldly matters such as politics will also be attractive to these people. However, if this area is flat and feels bony to the touch, then the subject probably lacks staying power and may not be able to cope with too much going on at any one time in their lives.

Notice how the fingers "sit" on the top of the palm. If they form a gentle arch, with the first and fourth fingers reasonably level, there will be neither excessive aggression nor undue diffidence. Good old-fashioned common sense tends to predominate in these individuals.

If the fingers are evenly set and well formed there will be no lack of confidence. Indeed, this person is likely to be so self-assured that he or she refuses to make time for anyone else's opinions.

LEFT The top zone reveals ambitions and ideals. The bottom (material) zone denotes your primary desires. The zone in the middle reflects the balance between the two.

ABOVE A healthy middle zone shows someone with an especially good eye for a bargain.

THE FINGERS

★ ★ ★ ★ ★ ★ ★ ★ ★ ★ ★ ★ ★ ★ ★ ★ ★

THE APPEARANCE, SHAPE, position, and development of the fingers, individually or collectively, are indicators of character and should be observed from both the back and front of the hand. Fingertips are also important and should be included in your overall analysis. (When assessing fingertips, ensure you are not misled by nail shapes.)

The inclination and length of one finger in relation to another, and the overall length in comparison to the palm, are important. Finger joints should be observed to see if they are smooth or knotted, and the knuckles should also be assessed.

Always look at both hands and compare each finger with its counterpart on the other hand. There are often surprising differences which may account for personality traits you are initially unable to understand.

RIGHT Critical types have knotted top joints; if both joints are knotted you have identified a true skeptic.

SMOOTH FINGERS

Smooth fingers indicate versatility and an easygoing or intuitive nature. Short fingers suggest an impulsive streak, someone who knows instinctively what to do and who will forge ahead before fully grasping the intricacies of a situation. Long-fingered people thrive on complex, detailed work and they take time to assimilate everything before acting. They may still be impulsive but are more adaptable and versatile.

BELOW Smooth fingers denote a versatile character who is easygoing.

smooth fingers

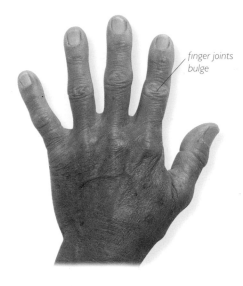

finger joints bulge

KNOTTED FINGERS

Bulges or knots at the joints should be regarded as checkpoints, places where incoming information is stopped and checked. Knotting at each of the joints implies a critical nature, one who must examine every angle of a situation before making a decision or taking action.

Prominent top joints indicate a slow nature, one often difficult to please. They may worry unnecessarily, which creates nervous tension. These people are likely to perform poorly at interviews, even when they know exactly what is expected of them.

Knotted lower joints make people more pragmatic and methodical. Tidy and rather conservative in their overall approach to life, they are keen on personal discipline.

When both joints are prominent, the person is a true skeptic. Often obsessively neat and tidy, they are logical in the extreme. They may be involved in more than one task at a time, but move from one to another as their mood changes. They are very difficult to please, and choose to live in a quiet, studious environment.

A narrow gap here shows insecurity.

A low-set little finger denotes feelings of inferiority.

SPACING

A wide gap between the first and second fingers shows confidence and a love of independence, especially in thinking. This person is not one of the herd and will act and behave as he or she sees fit. A narrow space suggests the owner is likely to keep their thoughts private, but still go along with the majority.

A wide space between the second and third fingers suggests an inability to plan for the future – the type who exists from day to day. If narrow, however, the owner nearly always has tomorrow in mind. He or she will save for a rainy day and have a strong concern with personal security and safety.

A wide space between the third and fourth fingers denotes those who prefer to act on their own. They can be quite impatient if they are part of a group that cannot make decisions and may adopt a solitary, independent stance. Conversely, a narrow space is the hallmark of a follower – there is a lack of confidence and a need for constant reassurance.

Flexible fingers suggest a flexible mind, a good nature, someone eager to please. With stiff or unyielding fingers expect to find a similar personality, but with a selfish streak thrown in for good measure. Fingers that are collectively flexible between the middle and base phalanges suggest practicality and common sense.

This wide space shows independence.

When the knuckles bend back easily the owner is adaptable, acts quickly and sensibly, and is often reliable in emergencies as well as other potentially stressful situations.

THE SETTING

When the fingers are evenly set along the top of the palm the owner is usually well balanced, taking the rough with the smooth without getting unduly upset.

As a rule, the index and little finger are slightly more low-set than the others. A very low-set first finger reflects a lack of self-confidence and even a somewhat withdrawn, unassertive personality. When the little finger is very low-set there is an inferiority complex. These people have difficulty expressing their emotional needs and do not trust others easily. They may avoid socializing as a result.

THE FIRST FINGER

The first finger, also known as the index finger, represents the id, the ego, ambition, and pride in the self. The straighter the finger, the stronger these characteristics. If the finger is slightly bent the owner is likely to be rather cautious and mistrustful.

When the first finger is shorter than the third, the owner can be hard, cold, and intolerant of personal restrictions. They dislike criticism, no matter how well meant, but they are often harsh critics themselves.

LEFT If the fingers are bunched together, you are gregarious; wide spacing denotes an extrovert.

ABOVE People with a wide space between their third and their fourth fingers tend to act independently and may be loners like this little girl.

LEFT Spacing between individual fingers should be checked. Ambition, for example, will be denoted by the Jupiter finger standing apart.

A first finger longer than the third finger denotes pride, ambition, and plenty of self-confidence. A prominent first or top joint indicates a skeptical nature; a prominent second joint suggests good self-discipline. When the first finger knuckle is pronounced, expect to find a tidy mind in a tidy body.

A stiff first fingertip shows a stubborn streak, while a flexible tip shows versatility. A round or conic fingertip suggests an impressionable and intuitive nature. A square tip is an indication of a conventional outlook and is likely to belong to a disciplinarian, but one with good practical leadership skills. The owner of a spatulate tip is also a determined leader, an active person who will take charge at any cost.

When the first phalange is long there is natural intuition; if it is short, materialism is indicated. If thick, it suggests selfishness; if thin, austerity.

If the second phalange is long, the person will be materialistic but in a constructive way; if short, there is probably a lack of ambition. A thick second phalange implies selfishness and a love of physical comfort, while a thin one suggests ambition. If the second phalange is extremely thin, the person might be reckless, a loose cannon.

A long basal phalange shows a proud and dictatorial approach to life; if it is short, there is a matter-of-fact attitude. A thick basal phalange suggests greed and a high sex drive; if thin, they tend to be prudish.

THE MIDDLE FINGER

This finger, usually slightly longer than the others, is the balance finger – a normal-length middle finger suggests a well-balanced personality. If this finger is excessively long, the owner may be a lonely and overly serious person. A shorter-than-average middle finger indicates one who promises much but often delivers little or nothing. There may be a gambling streak.

If the middle and first fingers are of equal length, expect to find a scholarly outlook with little or no sense of humor. People whose middle and third fingers are the same length tend to take too many risks and may have problems in business matters.

Idealists possess a thin third finger.

A conic tip suggests humor.

Those with a long middle finger tend to be loners.

A square tip suggests a disciplined personality.

A short first finger indicates coldness and intolerance of others.

A prominent first or top joint may counterbalance the natural tendencies of the finger. A prominent second phalange joint shows practicality in day-to-day affairs. When this finger's knuckle is prominent, there is an orderly and tidy approach to life in general.

A conic tip to this finger suggests a dry sense of humor, while a pointed fingertip indicates an overoptimistic nature. A spatulate tip on the middle finger, however, suggests a pessimistic person with a rather solemn outlook. A square tip denotes a strict disciplinarian and moralist.

Those whose middle finger has a long first phalange will usually have a prudent nature and possibly lack a sense of humor.

Those with a short top phalange tend to be followers with a calm, steady nature. If the phalange is thick there may be a lack of refinement; if thin, the person may have a questioning or mistrustful approach.

A long second phalange denotes a love of the outdoors, while a short one shows

A short fourth finger belongs to someone who lacks self-confidence.

unreliability. Those in whom this phalange is thick delight in outdoor pursuits such as gardening. A thin phalange suggests a scientific or possibly an unimaginative outlook.

A long basal phalange suggests the owner is inclined to be unreliable, perhaps with a touch of selfishness. A short section here implies a selfish or miserly type. A thick basal phalange denotes someone who is sociable, if somewhat cautious or serious. A thin phalange can be an indication of an extremely unsociable and solitary nature.

THE THIRD FINGER

This finger indicates artistic tendencies. Whatever sense of realism and practicality the owner may possess is usually conditioned by the individual facets of the third finger.

A longer than average finger implies strong practical artistic talents. Occasionally there may be a gambling streak. When longer than the first finger, the owner is a creative and innately happy soul. A short finger indicates a pessimistic nature, with little if any artistic inclination or creativity.

A straight third finger emphasizes artistic qualities. If this finger inclines toward the middle finger, any artistic inclinations will be combined with business ability. If it leans toward the little finger, the owner probably makes money in an arts-related field.

LEFT The middle, or Saturn, finger denotes balance and understanding. If it is short expect promises to be broken.

ABOVE A love of the outdoors is often identified by a long second phalange in the middle finger.

RIGHT The third finger denotes creativity and artistic tendencies. If it leans toward the middle finger expect artistic leanings to be combined with business acumen.

A spatulate tip marks the instinctive entertainer, whether an amateur or a professional. The square tip shows a love of wealth and comfort, while a pointed tip implies a born idealist. The round or conic tip indicates a talent that may not be fully exploited or developed.

A prominent first joint suggests a natural critic; a noticeable second joint indicates a strong sense of form. A prominent knuckle also denotes a sense of form and artistic flair.

A long first phalange signifies creativity, but the longer it is, the more pretentious the owner is likely to be. A short phalange denotes a lack of artistic or literary interest and ability. When this phalange is thick, expect to find a more down-to-earth attitude in art; if it is thin, the person is probably a purist or an idealist.

A long second phalange accompanies an inspired approach to art, but a short one indicates little or no attraction at all to the arts. A thick phalange indicates practical creativity; when this area is thin, there is usually a poor appreciation of form or shape.

The subject with a long basal phalange will be materialistic and avaricious. A short phalange indicates a lack of artistic appreciation. For those with a thick phalange, personal comforts come first, while a thin one shows self-sufficiency.

ABOVE Painting might be one way that a particularly creative character might express him- or herself. Creativity is denoted by the length and shape of the third finger.

THE FOURTH FINGER

If the little finger reaches or goes beyond the nail phalange of the third finger, it is considered long. Owners of a long fourth finger often use the instinctive side of their nature to communicate effectively, and enjoy social and business exchanges.

A short finger implies poor self-expression, and a low-set one always indicates a lack of self-confidence – these folks tend to follow the crowd.

People with a prominent top joint are highly expressive communicators. A well-developed second joint shows precision and caution in business and commercial matters. Those with a prominent knuckle dislike being surrounded by untidiness and clutter.

A spatulate tip on this finger is the sign of a practical and creative craftsman. A conic or round tip indicates a good sense of humor, as does a pointed tip. A very pointed tip shows an adventurous spirit unable to refuse a dare or challenge – these people will heartily enjoy adventures. A square tip indicates a natural teacher, someone easily able to translate theory into practice.

A supple fourth finger is a sign of a flexible mind and social life, while a stiff finger shows strong social responsibilities and a preference for sticking to the rules.

A long first phalange on the fourth finger indicates perception, eloquence, and a good investigative mind. This finger is likely to be found on a lawyer or even a novelist. A fairly slow and basic approach to life is indicated by a thick first phalange.

Those who have a long second phalange display practical commercial understanding; a short second phalange is characteristic of a reasonably average but loyal character. A thick phalange here suggests a lack of scruples, one prepared to bend the rules to achieve his or her desires. A thin section implies a financially astute business type.

People with a long third phalange can talk the hind legs off a donkey and sell anything to anyone, but they may not always be as honest with themselves as they should be. A short section here indicates one who is easily led by others. A thick phalange implies poor moral standards and a misplaced personal vanity. A thin base section can show poor imagination and little zest for living.

When classifying and interpreting finger types on the one hand you must remember to compare them with their counterpart on the other hand. You will find that there are often surprising differences between them that may be the source of some personality traits that you are initially unable to understand.

LEFT Those with a long fourth finger are instinctive and communicative; a short finger denotes an inability to express yourself.

ABOVE A pointed tip on the fourth finger belongs to the type of person who simply can't refuse a challenge and seeks excitement and adventure.

THE KNUCKLES

These are actually the third joints of the fingers and are indicators of personal appearance, health, and hygiene. When the knuckles all look fairly even, the owner usually has a special knack for always looking neat and tidy. These people are often concerned with diet and personal fitness.

People with uneven knuckles may appear to be neat and tidy, but this is generally superficial. As a rule only the middle finger is prominent, in which case the owner will pay only lip service to personal hygiene, appearance, or possessions. Open a drawer or lift a cushion, and the person's true carelessness and disorganization will be revealed. These are the people who make a performance out of searching through their pockets or purses for keys or change.

A clean and tidy person possesses even knuckles.

Those with uneven knuckles can be careless and disorganized.

BELOW A palmist checks the knuckles for indications of personal appearance.

THE THUMB

* * * * * * * * * * * * * * * *

THE THUMB IS the most important feature of the hand, for its ability to work in opposition to the fingers places human beings above all other animals. Having a truly opposable thumb has allowed human beings to grasp and manipulate tools and other objects in ways that no other mammal can.

In palmistry the thumb is a principal key to the character. It represents behavior, purpose, vitality, willpower, reason, and logic. It shows whether one is a leader or a follower. In Eastern palmistry it is considered most important in delineating the character.

The right and left thumbs frequently differ, even if only slightly, so any assessment of the thumbs must be done with care. Each thumb should be judged not just in relation to the hand on which it is found, but also in comparison with the other hand and thumb. Often a weak right thumb will be offset by a strong left one, or vice versa. So, always check both thumbs carefully.

A strong left thumb with a weak right hand indicates problems in persuading others or initiating projects, but a strong right thumb partnered by a weak left hand indicates a strong character that has developed over the years.

RIGHT The thumb indicates character; a strong thumb is important but it may denote stubbornness.

BELOW The thumb is an extremely expressive part of the hand and is distinctive to humans. Because it is opposable, it allows us to grasp and manipulate objects with great dexterity.

A strong thumb reaches half way up the basal phalange of the first finger.

Two strong thumbs show a stubborn, "difficult" type, someone who prefers straight-forward facts and isn't easily swayed by sweet talk. Two weak thumbs indicate a changeable character who bends with the wind and lacks consistency.

LENGTH

The length of the thumb should be approximately the same as that of the little finger on the same hand. When held close to the hand, the thumb's tip should reach at least half-way up the basal phalange of the first finger on the hand on which it appears. If it does not do so, it is referred to by palmists as a short or weak thumb.

A long thumb suggests a love of being in command and good managerial ability. If the thumb is overlong, the person may be determined and stubborn. A short thumb represents the exact opposite of a long thumb. A long first phalange suggests a bully who in extreme cases can be a willful tyrant. A long middle phalange is found on people who must reason everything out before taking action. Unfortunately, by the time these folk reach a decision, it may be far too late to take effect.

A long, well-developed third phalange or Venus mount suggests strong physical appetites that may possibly interfere with

The average angle of the thumb – in relation to the other fingers – is 45 to 90 degrees.

normal social life. A thin, lean phalange indicates introversion and prudery.

ALIGNMENT

When held naturally, the thumb either aligns with the fingers or opposes them. A thumb that aligns with the fingers shows a spontaneous nature, someone who prefers to pursue pleasure rather than fulfill obligations.

When the thumb opposes the fingers it will be difficult to get to know the owner intimately, for though this person may seem open, in fact just the opposite is true. He or she is likely to have a wide range of acquaintances from all walks of life, but few, if any, will be allowed to become an intimate and close friend. If this person's trust is ever broken, the relationship will never be the same again. It is also extremely difficult to predict how such a person will react in a given set of circumstances. More often than not there will be signs of inner conflict elsewhere in the hands.

ANGLES

When the hand is in a relaxed position there should be at least a 45-degree angle between the thumb and the index finger. An angle less than this is considered narrow and suggests a small-minded, prejudiced view of life, accompanied by poor perception,

limited responses, and selfishness. An angle greater than 90 degrees shows resolve and leadership qualities. Anything between 45 and 90 degrees is considered about average.

Sometimes the edge of the basal phalange may appear more angular than curved, and there may be one or two angles formed between the wrist and the second phalange. These are known as the angles of time: the top one gives a sense of rhythm and the lower one a sense of harmony. One can be present without the other. Either way, they add to the subject's sense of rhythm in movement, either in dance or in sport, or in the sense of the creative flow of a writer or musician.

When both angles are present there will be an appreciation of time in everyday matters. People who study human behavior – as an amateur or professional – also often have both angles and the accompanying sense of the importance of timekeeping.

LEFT The thumb is usually angled between 45 and 90 degrees from the index finger. If greater, the subject will have leadership qualities. A narrow angle suggests someone who is narrow-minded.

BELOW Angles at the edge of the basal phalange of the thumb denote rhythm and harmony. They often show in the hands of dancers and musicians.

POSITION

The lower the thumb is set on the side of the hand the more the inspirational side of the character will show through. Should a low-set thumb be combined with a wider than usual angle, expect to find an adventurer or great explorer, someone to whom a nine-to-five job would be a total anathema. If the angle is narrow, the subject's main concern in life will be self-preservation, no matter what he or she does.

A high-set thumb indicates a clearly defined and largely instinctive creative flair. Someone with a narrow angle and a high-set thumb is inclined to bend the rules rather than break them, and to do it with skill. If a high-set thumb is also aligned with the fingers, expect to find a person who will drop everything at the first opportunity to set off in search of a new adventure. Some of these people, in fact, hardly have a sensible bone in their body!

FLEXIBILITY

Examine the thumb for flexibility. A supple, flexible tip implies an impulsive nature, the sort of person who will vary his or her attitude just to relieve boredom. A more rigid tip suggests a strict disciplinarian, a stubborn person who may not be able to compromise. Difficult to understand, such people are hard to work with, and living with them demands inexhaustible patience.

ABOVE Explorers or adventurers usually have a low-set thumb at a wider than 90 degree angle to the palm.

RIGHT As well as checking the thumb's angle, look at the finger tip for flexibility – if it is rigid the subject is keen on discipline.

Test the flexibility and consider the thumb's angle at the same time.

Stretch back the tip of the thumb to test its flexibility.

THE TIP OF THE THUMB

When the tip of the thumb bends outward, the subject will usually have a more than generous streak and a receptive mind. Should the tip turn inward, however, the owner will generally be petty, mean, and selfish.

A square tip suggests a realist. Though they may be hard taskmasters, these people prefer to lead by example and usually have a sense of fair play. For example, they would be unlikely to ask people who work for them to do something they themselves cannot do.

People who have a bulbous top to their thumbs have strong appetites and tend to live a very physical life. What they want, they have. It is futile, and sometimes dangerous, to try to oppose them. These folks have a dreadful temper and are capable of blind fury. However, when they do explode, the outburst is likely to be over almost as soon as it starts. Take care in your dealings with such people – they can be utterly ruthless pursuing their aims.

The thumb with a spatulate tip is the sign of the craftsman, a practical person who knows instinctively how to get things done. People with a round or conic tip respond easily (too easily at times) to external stimuli. A pointed tip indicates an idealistic or indecisive type. This personality can appear submissive, but do not be fooled – though they may seem weak, they usually have a knack for spotting the weaknesses in others and seizing the advantage for themselves.

The "spokeshave" thumb tip tapers toward the top and is best viewed from the side. People with this shape thumb tip have an uncanny ability for getting others to do things they might not ordinarily do. Afterward, when their motives are questioned, they will probably just shrug their shoulders and smile.

The tip of the thumb bending outward denotes a realist.

Energetic, physical types have a thumb with a bulbous tip.

Those with the "spokeshave" thumb tip are persuasive.

LEFT If the tip of the thumb bends inward, rather than outward, expect a mean and petty-minded character.

LEFT Watch out for those with a bulbous tip to their thumb, they have a terrible temper and can be ruthless.

BELOW The subject with the "spokeshave" thumb may be persuasive but they will not necessarily have any motives.

THE BACK OF THE HAND

* * * * * * * * * * * * * * * * *

YOU CAN PRACTICE palmistry anywhere and anytime, simply by observing the backs of people's hands. This will not give you a complete reading, of course, but even a quick appraisal of the backs of the hands can provide a great deal of information.

When you meet someone for the first time, note the general skin color, length, and breadth of the backs of the hands. Look at the nails, too – not just for their individual shape, but also how they are kept.

NAILS

Nails are important; they indicate the temperament and the current state of health. They show stress or strain, nervous tension, and, sometimes, vascular problems. In fact, it pays to keep an eye on your own nails if you're under stress and note any changes.

Physically, nails are made of a hornlike substance called keratin and take about six months to grow from their hidden roots. Throughout the process any mark on a nail takes a corresponding time to grow out. Therefore, noting where on the nails particular marks occur may help to date certain recent illnesses. However, this doesn't apply to horizontal barring or longitudinal ridging, which may appear anytime the human system is under stain or stress. The most likely cause of ridging or barring in the nails is poor health caused by endocrine, glandular, or organic imbalance.

Bitten nails always relate in some way to an emotional cause that has resulted in behavior patterns not normally associated with the owner. White spots in a nail, which can cause brittleness, indicate a mineral deficiency that should be treated medically. Traditionally, white spots are said to refer to old love affairs the subject cannot entirely forget. The ancients also said that the nail may describe the former partner. On the Mercury finger, it implies a business or traveling type, on the third finger, an artistic type. If the white spots occur on the nail of the middle finger, the alliance may have been with an older partner; if they're on the first finger, the lover might have been a teacher.

Note the moons at the base of the nail; no moons at all suggests a weak constitution. (Moons can disappear, which can be an early warning of ill health somewhere in the body.) Good, clear moons speak of good health and a happy disposition. A bluish tinge to the moons can imply vascular trouble, while a yellowish hue suggests liver or kidney problems. Pale moons are often an indication of anemia, and a really white nail emphasizes this. It also suggests a basically cold nature with a strong selfish streak. Naturally red nails show a strong temper, which you'd do well to avoid arousing!

Nail shapes are an indication of character and personality, and palmists recognize four basic shapes: broad or narrow, long or short. Of course, there are many variations.

Square or slightly rectangular nails are found on people who are slow to anger and who also feel things very deeply. The small square nail suggests narrow-mindedess, someone who lacks any real depth of feeling. Large square nails belong to people who are not very forgiving if they are unnecessarily disturbed in some way. These folks may seem to forget, but they rarely forgive.

Nail with moons.

Nail without moons.

Nail with a white spot.

Nail with ridging.

Bitten nail.

Red/ridged nail.

Narrow nails show delicate health and, if they have a slight bluish tinge, weakness in the vascular system. Because the people who have these nails are so prone to upset, they are likely to have difficulties with their diet.

People with "filbert" nails are generally slow to anger. They may prefer to avoid problems, hoping they'll go away. Such people often lack energy and frequently indulge their lazy streak.

Owners of almond-shaped nails have refined and esthetic personalities. Naturally courteous, they have good taste and appreciate the better things in life. They make excellent, steadfast, and loyal friends. If they ever do lose their temper, it is expressed as an hysterical outburst.

A talon-shaped nail is a sign of a poor diet that has disturbed bodily functions. Assertive and slightly selfish, these folks take what they want. However, when all is said and done, these people are survivors.

Those with shell-shaped nails may also suffer poor health, are rather sensitive, and may be prone to nervous problems. Nails may grow into this shape, and when this happens, it is a message to the owner to slow down a little – or else!

Two other fairly common nail types are the dish-shaped or concave and its reverse, the curved or convex. The first type indicates poor blood supply or glandular problems brought about by a shock to the system. When such a shock occurs, the weakest point in the body is usually the first to give way. The curved nail almost always indicates respiratory weaknesses. Heavy smokers can develop this type of nail. People with severely curved nails may be tubercular.

Generally speaking, those with short wide nails, whatever their basic shape, have a critical nature, while people with longer nails tend to be far more tolerant and easygoing. Bitten nails almost always mean poor emotional balance, irritability, intolerance, and some inner sense of loneliness.

A wide gap between the end of the nail and the fingertip indicates a quick, violent temper. These folks explode but it is often all over almost as soon as it starts.

Square nail.

Shell-shaped nail.

Almond nail.

Talon-shaped nail.

THE COLOR OF THE HANDS

The amount and quality of the blood flow affects the hand's appearance, particularly its color. When circulation is poor, the blood will only partially perform its proper function, and general health will be impaired. This can affect temperament.

A dead-white hand that gives the appearance of lack of blood (as opposed to one that simply has very fair skin) reveals a character with a cold nature who lacks normal enthusiasm and passion for life. They may seem distant, shying away from an active social life and making little effort to please others, even those that are really close to them. They show little sympathy when things go wrong for others, and they do not seek or expect any sympathy for themselves, either.

A yellowish color to the hands is often associated with poor kidney function, but there can be other reasons for it. The yellow color may indicate a heavy smoker or someone who comes into contact with certain toxins or food additives. Very occasionally you may encounter a health-food fanatic who ingests high levels of carotene, either in the form of raw carrots or juice. People with a higher than average blood fat level also tend to have yellowish hands. Traditionally, the yellow hand is associated with an overactive bile flow.

The blue or purplish hand shows poor blood circulation, sometimes accompanied by poor localized blood pressure. As people grow older their responses to heat and cold become restricted and their reactions generally slow down. Hands and feet are the first to feel the difference. When determining the meaning of a blue hand, always look to the nails for further clues regarding health.

As far as character and personality are concerned, a blue hand often suggests somewhat slow mental and physical response rates.

A yellowish color to the hand may be a sign of unhealthy kidneys.

A sunburned hand would suggest a love of the outdoors.

A blue color in the hands may suggest poor circulation.

As a rule, people with red hands have abundant good health. Their thought processes tend to be slow, with poor initial perception but they are full of energy, enthusiasm, and purpose and they seem unable to do anything by halves. They are big eaters, for they need a lot of fuel to feed their intense, industrious natures. Their diet may not be particularly balanced, but what they eat is of no importance because they generally burn up the energy very quickly. They are overassertive to the point of aggression, and usually materialistic. Despite their uncomplicated approach to life they are loyal to those who show kindness and consideration.

The hand that is a normal, healthy pink color at room temperature indicates a normal, generally well-adjusted and balanced personality. Usually vivacious, generous, tender, and emotionally responsive, these people are a social asset in a group.

Skin that looks sunburned or weather-beaten shows a love of the outdoors; similarly, a rough skin texture often reveals an attraction to outdoor pursuits. Someone whose hand is also a basic square shape is likely to be a craftsman who prefers to work outdoors. A wide back to the hand may also indicate a love of the outdoor life.

The more narrow, smooth, pale hand with a soft texture is the sign of someone who prefers staying indoors.

Red hands show abundant good health.

LEFT The color of a person's hand can tell you a great deal about their general health and lifestyle.

PART TWO

THE MAJOR LINES
OF THE HAND

★ ★ ★ ★ ★

The main palmar lines – head, life, and heart – begin forming in the womb. As early as 20 weeks the hand may start to show basic markings. These lines have been proven to have genetic connections.

As personality and character develop, the lines alter to reflect the way the person matures. Weaknesses may be indicated by poor or faint markings, strengths by strongly etched lines. Hand markings can even relate to specific events that have had a powerful effect on the subject.

ABOVE The major lines of the hands begin to form in the womb and you will find that characteristics passed down the generations are reflected in the hand.

Experienced hand analysts can often trace the development of a subject's character and personality over the years; they look for certain places where such events have left their mark on the hand.

If a palmist can establish a subject's characteristics and pick out salient events from the past, he or she will be able to suggest fairly accurately how they may react to future circumstances. Do check both hands very carefully before making any pronouncements.

LEFT OR RIGHT HAND?

THROUGHOUT HISTORY, MANY cultures and civilizations have regarded the left hand as inferior, sinister, or evil. The word sinister, in fact, is Latin for "left." Even today there are people who regard left-handedness as inferior.

Because the left hand has always been associated with evil and bad luck, the right hand has naturally assumed the dominant and more favored position. This is frequently emphasized in the holy texts of various world religions. The Bible, for example, contains references to left and right hands, always associating the right with good, the left with weakness and deceit.

There are some people who still try to correct youngsters who are naturally left-handed, a practice that nearly always has negative psychological effects. Trying to suppress or change a child's natural hand preference can create a behavioral imbalance.

Why should some people be left-handed and others right-handed? To date, there is no valid technical or rational explanation. Generally speaking, the more developed hemisphere of the brain is the left, which corresponds with the right side of the body and therefore the right hand, but the left hemisphere of the brain is the more developed of the two hemispheres, even in left-handed people. The left hemisphere controls two very important cognitive skills, those of reading and writing.

Medical research shows that the left hemisphere of the brain controls and defines judgment and intelligence and that the right hand, by its shape, mounts, lines, and dermatoglyphics, reflects our basic character and personality. But modern palmists also acknowledge the right hand to be the dominant hand, irrespective of handedness in the subject.

The rules of palmistry state that our hereditary traits and inherent gifts are placed in our left hand, while the right hand reveals how well we develop these natural talents. The temptation is to reverse this when dealing with left-handed people. Examine both hands carefully before making any judgments and stick to the basic principles when dealing with left-handed people.

We cannot leave the subject of handedness without mentioning those who are ambidextrous. Theoretically, such people can use either hand to do anything with equal facility. In reality, however, almost no one is truly ambidextrous. Some people may simply find it easy to do some things with one hand and other things with the other hand. Many people, for example, who prefer to throw with the right hand are often more comfortable using their left hand in other activities. Only a few people can genuinely write, eat, brush their teeth, swing a bat, and perform myriad other activities equally well with either hand.

Almost everyone has a preference for one hand over the other, and often a child's inability to learn or respond to certain activities can be traced to his or her trying to use the wrong hand.

BELOW Left-handedness is still quite rare, amounting to an average of 10–20 percent of the world's population.

Thus, when reading hands, it is important to pay attention to left- or right-handedness or ambidexterity. Both hands must be studied anyway, but handedness can indicate how people may react or behave under stress or in an emergency. Remember, true ambidexterity is rare.

Examine the left hand first and then compare it with the right. Shapes can differ, and firmness and consistency frequently do. The lengths of fingers and their settings will not always exactly match, either.

Where two hands show few differences between them the owner almost certainly hasn't wanted to make changes in his or her life. He or she will have a fairly contented outlook, with an air of inner peace.

Where the hands are very different the subject may have had to overcome many difficulties to achieve his or her present place in life. The more dissimilar the hands, the more changes have been made by or imposed on the subject.

When the life lines display strong differences, it is usually because of domestic or environmental factors. In this case, it is possible that the subject was exposed to some kind of hardship in childhood, or such severe parental control or discipline that he or she wants to forget it. Sometime these differences may be related to health. In some cases both factors may be at work, interacting with each other.

Differing heart lines occur because of emotional problems, and the development, or lack of it, on each hand will confirm what the subject went through to reach his or her present state. If, for example, the person was

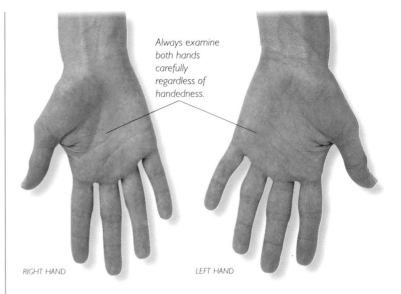

Always examine both hands carefully regardless of handedness.

RIGHT HAND   LEFT HAND

emotionally vulnerable and bullied, he or she would have had to adjust to the situation or remove themselves from it altogether.

Differences in minor lines could refer to changes in the subject's ambitions because of circumstances encountered in their life that forced or simply assisted the change.

The clearer the lines, the more even the subject's life is likely to have been. If you think of the lines on the palm as power cables then, whenever there is a break or other obstruction, the power is unable to flow smoothly. A line that divides or breaks implies a weakening of that line and, by inference, the sphere of life it refers to. If the line later reconnects, it is a sign that all is well again in that part of the subject's life.

Dots and crossbars on the palm lines are slightly less serious than breaks, but they also indicate a loss of energy in the line. Lines that fray or tasselate show the natural weakenings and the decline of energies we can all expect as we grow older.

ABOVE Hereditary gifts are usually placed in the lines of the left hand, while the right hand reveals personal development.

FULL OR EMPTY HAND?

* * * * * * * * * * * * * * * * *

A FULL HAND IS exactly that, full of an amazing tracery of lines that crisscross all over the surface of the palm. This pattern is indicative of a worrier. The mind is never still, and the subject finds it difficult to switch off and relax. There is always a remarkably active and vivid imagination. Such people are emotional, usually highly strung, and sensitive to a fault. There will always be a creative side to the person, possibly accompanied by a strangely philosophical approach to life.

A full hand contains a mesh of fine lines, as well as the major lines of the palm.

RIGHT The artist or creative type is likely to have a crisscross of lines all over the surface of his or her palms.

For some, this can represent a lack of confidence; these people seem to distrust the motives of those around them and for this reason they are often ill-at-ease. They are basically unhappy because they worry about upsetting people. Most tend to live on a razor's edge just waiting for this to happen, and as a result are rarely disappointed.

Often frustrated with jobs that require detailed or routine work, they do not take kindly to discipline but can bluff their way when they have to impose it. They are rarely the center of attention, but when they are they shine. They may end up in positions of authority quite early in life, for they know how to impress – they are perceptive, understanding, and often quite clever. Just as frequently, however, they lack initiative, and they are liable to lose out in the long term because they lack staying power. Though they look good when they are in full flow, they are ill at ease under the pressure that a position of power involves and this will take its toll on them.

The empty hand usually just has the three principal lines with a few small influence lines or marks dotted about here and there. People with this sort of hand seem not to feel things as deeply as full-handed folks, but if they do, they rarely show it. Not much excites them, and they refrain from unnecessary emotional displays. Steady and very reliable at whatever they do, they are tenacious and purposeful – once they start something, they will finish it!

It is unkindly said that these people are unintelligent. The truth, however, is that they are merely slow to react to ideas, and they take time to mull things over before giving a considered reaction. Once their minds are made up they go ahead, and whatever tasks they undertake will be done thoroughly and with care.

Empty-handed people are well suited for work that requires a disciplined approach. The armed services, for example, would be ideal for this type of person. They observe conventions and can give and take orders well. Almost always straightforward and without hang-ups, they are orderly and punctual and prefer a steady, quiet life. They can be creative and practical, and they often leave their mark – but somehow you just do not notice them easily.

It is relatively easy to assess whether a hand is "full" or "empty." But between these two extremes is the average hand, which can be more difficult to interpret. There is an approach, however, that makes it somewhat easier to discern the meanings in an average hand. Check if there are more horizontal lines going across the palm, or more vertical lines traveling upward from the wrist to the fingers. A greater number of vertical lines indicates a person who makes efforts at self-improvement. If there are more horizontal lines, the person is usually not geared up to deal adequately with life's problems. This can be because of an inability to look ahead and anticipate change, an inability to cope with the interference of others in their lives, or simply due to a lack of perception.

BELOW People with few lines on their hands are steady and reliable; this type of person would be suited to a life in the armed forces where discipline and compliance are expected.

An empty hand is characterized by three principal lines and very few fine lines.

THE HEAD LINE

★ ★ ★ ★ ★ ★ ★ ★ ★ ★ ★ ★ ★ ★ ★ ★ ★ ★

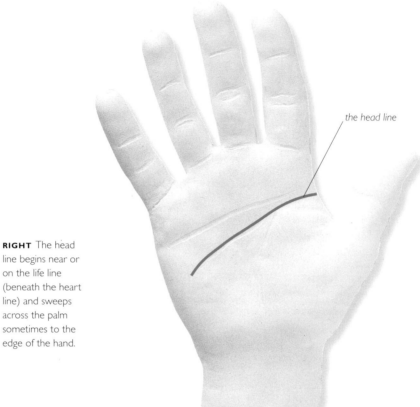

the head line

RIGHT The head line begins near or on the life line (beneath the heart line) and sweeps across the palm sometimes to the edge of the hand.

THE HEAD LINE is the most important of all the lines on the hand, for it reveals the quality of the subject's intelligence along with the control that their intelligence exercises over the rest of the body.

This line represents the way one thinks, reasons, and views the world. It also indicates perceptivity and how one applies all this mental power. The head line on the left hand refers to the innate qualities of the subject's mind, while the line on the right hand refers to the development and exploitation of those gifts, the conscious or active direction the subject has adopted.

The right-hand line shows personal levels of adaptability, and indicates how education and early circumstances have influenced personality. Any real differences between the hands reflect changes: the greater the differences, the more experienced the person.

When the lines on both hands are compared, one may seem lighter, less marked than the other. If the weaker line is in the right hand the subject is likely to have a negative personality. If the left-hand line is the weaker, the character is more positive, and the subject has used willpower to break away from any external influences that might be restrictive. If both lines are of equal intensity there will have been few changes in the subject's life, and there is generally little difference between the subject's inner nature and the way the subject actually presents himself or herself to the world.

THE IDEAL HEAD LINE

The ideal head line starts very near the line of life and sweeps out into the palmar surface, bowing or slightly sloping toward the top of the Luna mount to end under the Mercury finger or at the percussion itself. It should be clear of all influence marks other than the expected vertical lines that cross in a normal manner. There should be no dots, bars or cuts, islands, chaining, furring, or fraying. It may be deeply etched or only just be barely seen. This ideal line indicates good perceptive values with a reasonable approach to life largely governed by an uncluttered mind with a bright, intelligent outlook. The more the line slopes, the more imagination is brought into play.

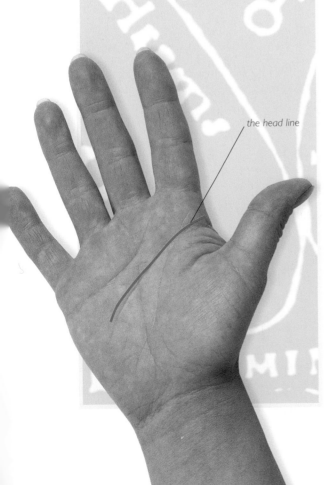

the head line

LEFT The longer the head line the more diversified the subject's thinking. Although – as Descartes' philosophy suggested – thinking defines human existence, we all think in different ways and this is reflected in the variety of identifiable head lines.

People think in many different ways, and it is only natural that we should adopt as many different approaches to life. Furthermore, any individual's attitudes and thought processes may vary at different times in his or her life, perhaps according to mood or situation. It is, therefore, reasonable to expect the head line to have a wide variety of different starting places.

The head line can start from anywhere on the Jupiter mount or inside the line of life, either just touching it or slightly away from it. It may travel across the zone of Mars, then dip slightly or slope very steeply, ending on the Luna mount. It may end suddenly, fork once or twice, fray, or tasselate. Any of the branches formed by a fork can take a new direction altogether to run that individual path to the end.

Different Head Lines

* * * * * * * * * * * * * * * * * *

A SHORT LINE on a conic hand with long fingers suggests that art and business combine well. For example, on the hand of a clothing designer whose styles appeal to a young, trendy market without being too outlandish or impractical. The longer head line indicates more imaginative and diversified thinking. People with long lines are more flexible than those with short lines, and certainly far more open to suggestion.

A long head line on a square hand can indicate a confusing combination of the imaginative and the practical. When decisions have to be made, the owner is likely to spend too much time looking for pitfalls that may not be there.

Long head lines are more suited to conic or pointed hands, which belong to people who are inherently more artistic and better able to follow through on imaginative ideas.

A Sydney line is a headline that extends from one side of the hand to the other, virtually cutting the hand in two. This line indicates excellent mental control and, if the rest of the hand implies an inflexible nature, the owner will also be selfish. A deeply etched line will emphasize this, while a faint line suggests one who is more easily swayed, particularly by an appeal to the emotions.

The higher the line starts on the first finger mount, the more honorable the person is likely to be both with others and himself or herself. If such a line is heavily etched, the owner loves flattery. The deeper the line, the more egotistical the owner.

The more level the rectangular shape between the head and heart lines, the more common sense prevails. The wider the gap

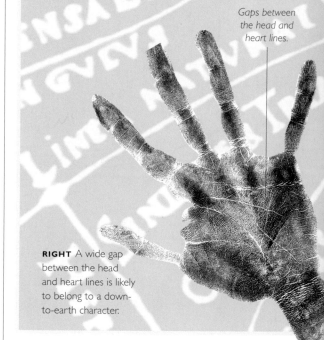

TYPES OF HEAD LINE

The shorter the head line, the more practical the subject; a line that reaches only to just below the middle finger shows a mind concerned with mundane matters. This line is usually seen on a square hand.

Gaps between the head and heart lines.

RIGHT A wide gap between the head and heart lines is likely to belong to a down-to-earth character.

between head and heart lines, the more practical and down to earth the person; the narrower the gap, the more emotional the character – decisions are hard for this type.

The wider the gap between the start of the head and life lines, the more impulsive the personality. Such people are ambitious, and confident of their ability to carry out their plans. However, they often antagonize others with their lack of tact and diplomacy.

The closer the source of the head line to that of the life line, the less confident and more conventional the person's spirit. These

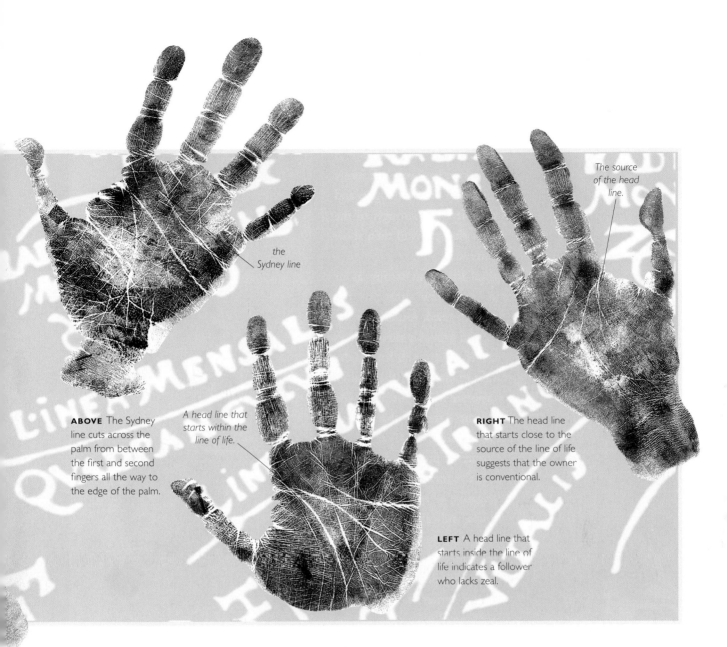

the
Sydney line

The source
of the head
line.

ABOVE The Sydney
line cuts across the
palm from between
the first and second
fingers all the way to
the edge of the palm.

*A head line that
starts within the
line of life.*

RIGHT The head line
that starts close to the
source of the line of life
suggests that the owner
is conventional.

LEFT A head line that
starts inside the line of
life indicates a follower
who lacks zeal.

folks can be tempted to bend the rules, but rarely to break them entirely. Reason and thinking are conditioned by their emotional responses to a situation.

A head line that starts from inside the life line is the sign of a follower, a person who lacks "push." He or she will be very cautious, unable or unwilling to take chances, and certainly will be no gambler.

When a head line rises toward the Mercury mount, the owner's nature can seem cold. When the line actually remains above the central line of the hand, it is as though all feeling and warmth is absent from personal contact. If such a line is found on both the subject's hands, the demands of the mind will always win out over other emotional considerations.

An island on any part of the head line suggests a weakening of the power of the whole line. If the island begins shortly after the start of the line and splits into a long island until just before the end of the line, the owner has probably kept secret certain private matters for the period represented by the island formation.

When the head line breaks, therefore, it indicates that the owner has been sufficiently motivated to pursue his or her thoughts and turn them into reality. The stronger of the two branches after the split will then show the dominant interest.

If the original line is as strong as or stronger than the new branch, the experiment has been tried, found wanting for some reason, and probably now receives only lip service. If the branch line is the stronger, the subject has liked the change enough to incorporate it into his or her life style, possibly to the extent of abandoning the old way of life entirely.

A fork that comes at the end of the head line suggests an active mentality that is best suited to investigative or research work. A fork on a long line indicates an ability to follow two careers, often quite different from each other, at the same time.

A shortish fork with one line that turns upward is called the "writer's hook," but its application is not limited to writing; it refers to any form of creative work. When one of these forks reaches the outer edge, the owner is likely to gain international recognition – whether this is fame or infamy will depend on the nature of his or her endeavors.

Occasionally you may find a double head line, but this rarely occurs on both hands. Usually found on the right hand, it indicates the ability to exist or work in two totally different spheres at the same time. The subject often takes steps to ensure that these two areas of his or her life remain separate and never meet, and few associates are aware of the other side to the person's life.

ABOVE The "writer's hook," found at the end of a forked head line, indicates a subject who is adept at any form of creative work.

RIGHT The source of the head line is close to that of the heart, which would suggest a conventional type.

FORKS IN THE HEAD LINE

A fork in any line always indicates contrasting or conflicting paths for the owner to consider. On the head line in particular it suggests dissatisfaction with the way the subject has lived his or her life. There is a need to try something different, if only for the experience.

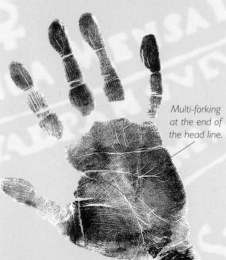

Multi-forking at the end of the head line.

ABOVE Forking at the end of the head line suggests a division between common sense and the imagination.

The head line's source is close to the heart line.

A head line that sweeps downward into the Luna mount shows an overactive imagination. The deeper the line moves into the mount, the less positive the mental faculties become. If the actual line fades these traits will be emphasized.

A chained, furry, or wavy head line suggests a low boredom threshold and lack of concentration. These people's efforts don't usually end well, so it is best not to put them in a responsible position. Although associates can help at first in the mistaken belief that they are assisting the person through teething troubles, they soon withdraw their support.

If the head line fades a little toward the end it indicates that the weakness that comes with age will take its toll on the subject. Anyone with this sort of line should slow down as they get older and relinquish certain aspects of their life gracefully. Unfortunately, such people don't take kindly to warnings to slow down. They should be tactfully asked to do so.

When the head line is much stronger-looking than the life line, physical activities are of secondary interest. The head rules, for these people are headstrong. They may have an excess of nervous energy, which may lead to a burnout of their physical reserves.

A thin or rather weak-looking head line that meanders over the palm implies a weak or unstable character. If the meandering line

a furred head line

ABOVE People with a furred head line have the misfortune of having a low boredom threshold.

is thick and heavy-looking, the owner will probably have a shallow nature. Should the head line contain both variations – a strong section followed by a weak line for a short while – the subject will show very poor self-discipline. This type is unable to cope in an emergency or sudden crisis, although this may be less the case if the palmar surface is firm or the overall skin texture is rough. A soft palm always implies a lazy streak in its owner.

A fine head line shows that work has to be carefully planned to include adequate rest periods. It is unwise for the subject with this type of line to sustain mental or physical effort for too long.

Wide and shallow lines imply a similar nature, but for different reasons. These people are good at what they do for as long as they are able to do it, but they lack staying power, and their perception levels may be less than average. Like a river where the bed is so visible it is easy to dam, if you put enough problems in the way of these people, their previous efforts are wasted because the line has insufficient power to overcome them.

Influence lines that rise from the head line always refer to the subject's efforts to improve his or her standing in either social or business relationships. Lines falling away from the head line indicate losses through poor decision-making at the time indicated by the position of the minor line.

ABOVE People with a fine head line have to remember to rest regularly, for although they have plenty of energy it tends to run out rather easily.

THE LIFE LINE

* * * * * * * * * * * * * * * * * *

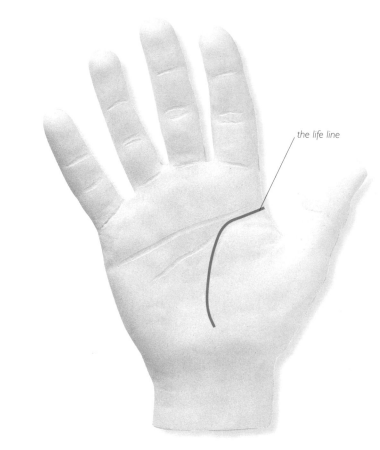

the life line

RIGHT The life line dips down and may curve around the base of the thumb.

BELOW Check your child's line of life for clues to his or her well-being.

A MAJOR MISCONCEPTION about palmistry is that a long life line indicates a long life and *vice versa*. Nothing could be further from the truth. People with a very short line of life have lived to a very old age, while others have died very young despite having a long life line. I have even seen hands with no life line at all, and while their owners may not be robust, they do lead full lives. Essentially, the life line reveals the quality of life, physical well-being, and the strength of the constitution. It is also a measure of energy, vitality, and endurance.

If the life line tightly encircles the ball of the thumb, it suggests a restrictive attitude and a lack of physical zeal in the subject. On a wide hand this can suggest limited activity, but on a narrow one it is an indication of a general lack of enthusiasm for anything – there is very little that will be a cause of excitement in these people. For them, a cool exterior and composed appearance will always be at hand.

The line can end in many ways. It may simply tail off, or it may fork into two, three, or more branches. It may fray or tasselate, or it can end quite abruptly.

The actual beginning of most life lines is hidden in the skin pattern at the edge of the hand, and a good-sized magnifying glass should be used to determine the exact nature of the line's start. It may begin simply as a single line, or in a series of what appear to be small islands, or even in an open chain formation. It may be tied in some way to the source of the head line.

Pinpoint the source of the life line.

THE IDEAL LIFE LINE

The life line may start anywhere on the mount of Jupiter or the mount of Mars on the radial side of the hand; it can even be the hand's dividing line.

It should sweep out into the palm, curving down firmly and gently around the base of the thumb. It can end almost anywhere short of the base of the palm: under the base of the thumb, on the mount of Venus, on the Neptune mount, or on the mount of Luna.

In view of what it represents, the life line should always have a healthy, unmarked look about it, and it should be free of any influence marks. The firmer and wider the sweep of the line, the greater the subject's vitality and zest for living.

a healthy life line

ABOVE The life line should be firm and should sweep gently out into the palm if it is to indicate a healthy, happy individual.

If it is a single line, the subject will be fairly self-reliant. A chained or furry formation, however, suggests too much dependence on others, especially in the formative years. If the line starts in a series of open-ended islands in a kind of chain formation, tradition holds that there is an element of mystery associated with the birth – illegitimacy is suspected or perhaps the birth was difficult. In one case, for example, it was discovered that the person had been born not at home or in a hospital but in a railroad car!

An islanded or chained beginning to the line almost always implies a history of childhood ailments and weaknesses. The longer the line continues in this fashion, the more likely that there will be recurring bouts of the original problems.

If the line starts on the mount of Jupiter, the subject's personality will have ambition stamped all over it. Little is allowed to get in this person's way. This is the mark of a leader – whether or not the person is a good leader can be determined by other marks or patterns on the hand.

A line that starts lower down, on the Mars negative mount, is the sign of a follower. There will always be an air of uncertainty or self-doubt about this person.

When the life line starts out tied to the head line, there will be restrictions, either at home or at school, in the person's early life for as long as the two lines continue together. This mark is common and occurs much more in the left hand than the right.

Many young people try to escape their childhood environment because they feel it is far too restrictive, and their hands often indicate this early struggle for independence. Parents might well be advised to have a quick look at their children's hands for clues to what the future might hold for their kids and the rest of the family. If there are signs of conflict, families can perhaps seek out or anticipate ways to ease constraints and avoid possible clashes between siblings and adults.

When the life line on the right hand sweeps out into the palm, there will be a sustained effort to attain personal freedom and self-expression; this type of person has an independent streak. The reverse suggests a person who cannot get out of a rut, who needs to be told what to do. The subject has

had to make the best of his or her lot and, as a rule, is well aware of his or her problems, and there will be "effort marks" elsewhere in the hand to support this (see box).

Any effort line toward the Jupiter mount suggests a strong desire to better one's personal circumstances. A line that moves toward the Saturn mount shows a subject who is prepared to take on more than their share of hard work.

An effort line to the Apollo mount usually suggests easy and early success. (It is just possible that this is a Sun line, a mark that will be discussed in greater detail on pages 86 and 87.) An influence line toward the Mercury mount shows a natural flair for business and commerce or all matters involved with communication.

When assessing these small marks, check the inside of the life line as well. Lines that stem from the mount of Venus usually have family connotations. If they cross the life

line, obstruction from family members may have occurred. A strong, heavily etched influence line on the mount that stops well before it gets to the life line shows a supporting influence, again from within the family. The owner will enjoy a shared loyalty with this person.

Scrutinize both hands; often the line of life in one hand may seem weak, tailing off and fading away before it reaches even halfway down the palm. This sort of line is generally found on both hands or just on the left hand, but rarely on the right hand only. If you look carefully, you will see a firmer downward line that starts from the head line, a little closer to the center of the palm. The line will then continue as if it were the life line. This is probably the second line of life and should be read as such.

If it is the latter – a clear second line of life – the palm registers the subject's ever increasing dissatisfaction with the family and their living arrangements while he or she was still living in the home. Perhaps the subject has previously been exposed to severe disciplinary controls or impossible parental demands that made living at home seem more and more of a struggle. Eventually, something snapped in this subject, and he or she finally gave up, moved out, and made a bid for independence.

EFFORT MARKS

Effort marks, or influence lines, are like little vertical hair lines rising up from the main line. Careful examination of each effort line – especially on the right hand – will show when, why, and in which direction the subject chose to go.

Both these hands show effort lines from the line of life.

ABOVE AND LEFT
Look out for effort lines stemming from the main lines; careful and tactful questioning of your subject may reveal the source and aim of their efforts.

Another line may be found inside the main line on either or both hands. This is the line of Mars, a "sister" line to the main line that adds strength and support to whatever the main line indicates. Occasionally this line may be as long as the main line and just as firmly etched, constituting, in effect, a double line of life. This formation always indicates that the owner leads a double life. The subject has simply chosen to live in two worlds at the same time.

At the midpoint of its path, the line of life can start to break up or take on a different appearance. It may look a little stronger or weaker because of influence lines that crisscross it. It may fork, fade, chain, or tasselate. As a rule, this halfway point corresponds with midlife, and its appearance indicates how the subject is dealing with this stage of his or her life. A clear line with no real change at the midpoint suggests the owner is living comfortably and managing well, taking the knocks as well as enjoying the good times.

In many cases the life line, formerly broadly etched, starts to thin a little. This suggests a slight weakening of resolve and easing in the subject's efforts to pursue a career or other significant life goals. This is a normal pattern that indicates approaching age and all that goes with it.

When the line appears to strengthen after formerly being a little weak, it reveals that the owner is making even more of an effort to keep up with things. How this effort is affecting the owner will show a little further down the line. If the line seems to break up,

ABOVE A second line of life might suggest difficulty living at home, such as impossible parental demands.

the subject has taken on more than he or she can handle and should ease back and slow down – or else!

About now the line will either begin to swing inward to end under the mount of Venus, or move even further out into the palm and end on the Luna mount. If the line swings inward, it indicates that at this time of life, the subject feels ready to ease back a little and enjoy his or her comforts. All this person wants is to return home as soon as possible and relax, safe and sound in his or her own environment. This is probably the only place the subject feels truly secure.

If, however, the line swings further out into the palm, there is an increased desire to experience even more of life, and a very

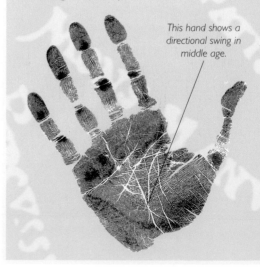

AGE AND THE LINE OF LIFE

It is possible to predict the direction of a subject's life and their response to the aging process. The line of life in the right hand will also change over the years.

This hand shows a directional swing in middle age.

strong wish to travel. If the line forks, there will be extreme restlessness. Look to see if there is any obstruction that might stop the subject from pursuing these yearnings. If there is none, the subject will almost certainly pack up and go, as if searching for his or her lost youth. There will be no stopping this character! This is a classic pattern for many people.

If the life line ends on the right hand Luna mount, but under the mount of Venus on the left, the owner loves travel but must return regularly to the security of home. When the line of life ends under the mount of Venus on the right hand, but on the Luna mount on the left, travel will be limited to reading books or watching television.

DIRECTION IN THE LINE OF LIFE

The line may show an obvious directional swing in one or both palms. It is important always to study and compare both hands carefully before completing an analysis.

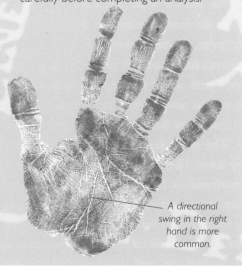

A directional swing in the right hand is more common.

The life line's energies are always weakened when obstructions occur. Any mark such as a dot, bar, chain, tasseling, or break impedes the flow of energy. An island shows a health problem or some inability to maintain the current life style – a stay away from their usual environment for as long as the island continues.

When the line regains its former appearance after any interruption or obstruction, the effect has been only temporary. If the line seems to look weaker after the interruption, the effect has registered and the hand has sent the owner a warning message.

Bars indicate setbacks over which the owner has little control. Dots signify worries and may have a nervous origin. Chaining in the line shows an overall weakening for as long as the configuration lasts. Sometimes it may appear as a series of small islands, which usually means recurring illness. A fraying or tasseling of the line shows that the subject's natural energy is liable to weaken with age, and the subject would do well to ease back gradually on his or her physical activities.

A circle or a semicircle anywhere on the life line suggests eye troubles. A square covering a break means an incident that takes its toll for a short while but from which the subject is likely to recover. A break in the line on both hands should always be viewed as serious. Care should be taken if the subject is planning anything hazardous.

ABOVE If the life line swings far out into the palm of the hand the subject probably has a strong yearning to travel.

islands on the life line

ABOVE Someone whose line of life shows an island may experience health problems or their expected life style will be impeded.

THE HEART LINE

★ ★ ★ ★ ★ ★ ★ ★ ★ ★ ★ ★ ★ ★ ★ ★ ★

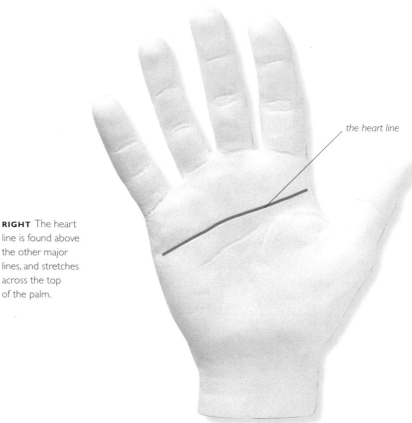

the heart line

RIGHT The heart line is found above the other major lines, and stretches across the top of the palm.

THE HEART LINE is associated with our emotions and how they color our character and personality. This line may also be used to assess some health problems, especially those that affect the vascular system.

If all emotion is instinctive rather than learned (and there are schools of thought that would dispute this), it seems logical to propose that the heart line should begin on the percussion side of the hand, anywhere under the Mercury finger. However, traditionalists maintain that the heart line must start on the radial side, beneath the index finger, where the other two principal palmar lines begin.

A third faction in this debate proposes that, because of what the line is said to represent, it cannot have a beginning or an end. This argument is supported by the fact that the line of heart frequently begins in a forked or multiforked formation, while the other lines usually end in one.

No matter what the hand shape, the lower the heart line reaches into the top of the palm, the more physically expressive the subject's nature is likely to be. The higher the line's path along the top of the hand, the more the owner will intellectualize and analyze his or her emotions.

The more deeply etched the heart line, the more likely that the subject will have emotional or health problems. (However, keep in mind that this line often seems dark in comparison with the other two major lines.) Any emotional or health defect should be backed up and confirmed by marks elsewhere in the hand; if it is not, the cause may be a purely physical one – for example, the vascular system affecting the health.

Check the nails, which are closely linked to the vascular system. Another possibility is that the subject has erratic or intense emotional responses to close relationships. Once again, check the nails, this time to see if they show longitudinal ridging. This indicates emotional tension, for which the cause may be located elsewhere in the hand.

A faint heart line suggests a cold, unemotional nature. Most of the subject's relationships will be purely physical. The subject may also be prone to an explosive and unpredictable temper. These people always have their feet planted firmly on the ground, and they are not easily fooled. Any attempt to trick or deceive them will be met with an unusually direct approach. Surprisingly, these people can also be fairly easygoing, but it is rare for them to allow the heart to rule the head.

If the heart line is set high on the palm with little or no curve in it, the owner is likely to be quite hard and cold. This will be especially so if the head line is also high on the palm. A narrow space between the two lines will reinforce this analysis.

A heart line that is set low in the palm implies an extremely passionate nature. Should both the heart and head lines be low-set, the subject is likely to be a possessive, jealous lover as well.

A wide gap between a low-set heart and the head line suggests that the head will rule the heart, but there will be frequent and unpredictable displays of temperament.

THE IDEAL HEART LINE

The ideal heart line starts on the Jupiter mount, follows a smooth curve under the fingers, and runs all the way to the outer edge of the hand with no influence marks interfering anywhere, apart from lines following their natural courses. Such a line would indicate an emotionally well-balanced individual with few if any real problems in this area.

Sometimes the heart line may start on the Saturn mount, or it may have a forked beginning with the branches commencing in any of the areas just mentioned. It may fuse with the head line to form one single line across the top of the palm, in which case it is called the Simian line. (see pages 90–91).

A heart line may be short or long, thick or thin. It may be heavily etched into the palm, or it may appear to be quite a faint marking. It might be chained, or have many little islands or lines throughout its length. It may be one big island from start to finish. In some cases it may not even be present at all! As you begin to study a greater variety of hands, you will discover how varied this line can be. Not surprisingly, it is considered a palmist's nightmare when it comes to analysis.

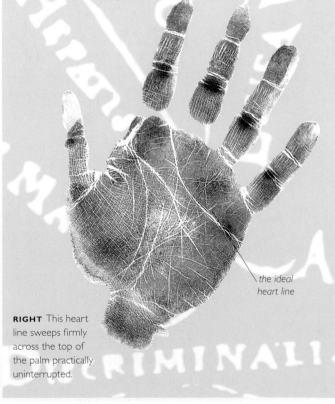

the ideal heart line

RIGHT This heart line sweeps firmly across the top of the palm practically uninterrupted.

The Source of the Heart Line

PERHAPS THE MOST frequently observed forked beginning to the heart line is one in which one branch originates from the Saturn mount and the other comes from the lower radial edge of the outer part of the Jupiter mount. The stronger of the two branches indicates which side of the nature dominates. If the line from the Jupiter mount is stronger, the subject has an honorable nature. Should the branch from the Saturn mount predominate, the subject's personality is refreshingly straightforward, open, and practical. This formation is often seen on the hands of people who care for others, such as social workers, nurses, and teachers. In many cases the owner chooses this sort of career so that he or she can care for people without getting too emotionally involved with them.

Occasionally you may see a heart line that appears to start with a three-pronged trident. Traditionalists consider this a very lucky formation.

Up to a point it can be lucky, but first check to see whether the lowest branch sends an influence line to the head line. If it does, the emotional outlook is rather negative. The subject may seem unable or unwilling to maintain a sound relationship for any length of time during their adult life.

When a line starts from the mount of Saturn and curves deeply into the palm to end on the percussion – more on the mount of Mars positive than on the Mercury mount – watch out. This type of person will quite

ABOVE Carers are likely to have a forked start to their heart line in which the branch from the Saturn mount is more prominent.

HEART LINE SOURCES

The higher the start of the heart line, and the higher it remains on the palm, the more idealistic the subject will be regarding anything to do with the emotions. If the line forks at the beginning, with one branch leading from the Jupiter mount and the other coming from the radial edge of the palm, the owner is generally emotionally adaptable and flexible.

heart line

head line

connecting lines

life line

ABOVE If the three principal lines are all connected, the subject can expect a serious trauma in their life.

RIGHT A heart line showing a lucky trident. Check that the lowest branch does not lean toward the the head line.

forked beginnings

ABOVE A forked heart line leading to the Jupiter and Saturn mounts. If the Saturn branch is strong, the subject is open.

lucky trident

dispassionately use people for his or her own ends. Cold and calculating, these individuals are often unable to understand or accept that other people have needs. As a result, they seem selfish in all their emotional dealings.

When the line begins on the extreme radial side of the hand, on the Mars negative mount between the thumb and the index finger, the owner almost certainly has a very possessive nature. The further the line reaches over to the other side of the hand, the less the owner will listen to criticism. It is almost impossible to shake this. Such people are motivated by what they see and hear, not by what others may say. If the heart line is fairly straight, this characteristic will be emphasized.

People on whom the line is set low over the palm have a softer approach and are able to readily admit mistakes when they have made them. Should the line be high-set, however, the owner will be cold, calculating, and extremely selfish. When such people have a task to do, the well-being of others is their last concern. You may be unable to appeal to their better nature because they probably don't have one!

When all three principal lines – head, life, and heart – are connected at their beginnings, it must be taken as a serious warning. At some time in his or her life the owner will experience a tremendous, even traumatic, shock to the system from which he or she will never really recover. This is the sort of event one never forgets, physically, mentally, or emotionally.

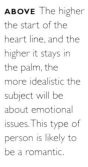

ABOVE The higher the start of the heart line, and the higher it stays in the palm, the more idealistic the subject will be about emotional issues. This type of person is likely to be a romantic.

The straighter the line, the more pragmatic and materialistic the owner's emotional approach. This person will have a firm resolve and take things as they come. People with straight heart lines are likely to be inhibited and rather awkward in emotional matters, tending to be cool and hard to get along with.

The subject with a curved heart line is far more receptive and accessible, with a much more flexible, imaginative approach. He or she is likely to have a much warmer, more demonstrative nature, and to be open to suggestion and possibility.

The square hand tends to have the straighter heart line. This explains why others sometimes suggest that these people are not very responsive emotionally. There is likely to be some truth in this; such people feel awkward about public displays of affection and avoid them.

THE RESTLESS HEART

Look closely at the beginning of the heart line that traditionalists agree is on the radial side of the palm. If there are small hairlike influence lines dropping away from the line or passing through it, the owner will be a restless type, someone who is constantly looking for something new to stimulate mind or body. This is not often seen on a square hand, but if it's seen on a conic hand it indicates a tremendous need for change. It is not unknown for people of this sort to vary a routine journey just for the sake of the change.

New faces and places are essential to keep their interest from flagging, but these people tend to have few really close friends. Instead they will have a wide and varied circle of acquaintances. Although they may seem to have broad general knowledge of a lot of things, often unusual subjects, their knowledge is mostly superficial. They can be very helpful, however, when you're trying to solve a crossword puzzle!

ABOVE People whose heart line shows restlessness need constant change. This type will be undaunted by frequent journeys to a variety of destinations.

LEFT Look at the heart line anywhere along its path to see if there are small hairlike lines leading away from it. They also indicate restlessness.

A heart line showing restlessness.

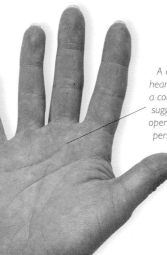

A curved heart line on a conic hand suggests an open, friendly personality.

A curved heart line on a square hand indicates a practical approach to relationships.

As a rule, the conic hand has a more curved heart line, and these personalities are more enthusiastic emotionally, and more demonstrative, open, and friendly. They are the ones who remember those nice little touches and gestures that mean so much. The more deeply etched the line, the stronger these characteristics will be.

A curved heart line on a square hand indicates a fairly down-to-earth approach to any emotional relationship. However, this is also likely to be accompanied by a high degree of sensitivity. Take great care with these people – they are so easily wounded by the wrong word or deed and they are likely to harbor their pain for some time.

A straight heart line on a conic hand denotes an owner who is likely to be inhibited but at the same time capable of extremely intense feelings. Deeply etched lines will reinforce this, while a shallow line suggests a cooler nature. Either way, these people are also extremely possessive and, as a rule, seek only their own gratification. In fact, once their passions are aroused they can become control freaks. A relationship with someone like this will feel quite one-sided to the partner. Very few see the real, inner person in such cases. These people do not trust readily, if at all.

It is essential to compare the heart lines on both hands. Where there are significant differences you can detect which way the subject now leans and determine what may have caused the change.

An intense-looking heart line on the left hand with a practical line on the right suggests that the owner may have been hurt in an earlier relationship. The reverse of this indicates a sympathetic partner who is probably understanding and has drawn the subject out of his or her shell. If there is no real difference between the two heart lines, the subject is likely to be content with his or her lot, neither seeking nor desiring any change. This person may dream, of course, but then, don't we all?

ABOVE A heart line should be read in relation to the shape of the hand.

BELOW The open and friendly character is likely to have a curved heart line in a conic hand.

The Heart Line and Health

* * * * * * * * * * * * * * * * *

The heart line should also be examined for its association with certain health factors. When looked at in conjunction with other features of the hand, the heart line's appearance will indicate current strengths and weaknesses.

Besides indicating problems in the vascular system, the heart line may also reflect certain dental problems, as well as difficulties with hearing, vision, and possible mineral deficiencies. Such problems will usually be indicated by small features like islands, chains, fraying, crosses, dots, bars (see pages 102–109), or unnecessary influence lines that cross through the path of the heart line.

An islanded heart line, or one made up of a small linked series of chains, indicates poor health related to the vascular system. If this line is found on the left hand only, with a firmer-looking line on the right hand, the subject's health will start to improve at the time shown. If the poorer line is on the right hand, partnered by a strong left-hand line, the health may start to falter at the time indicated in the right hand.

Many medical authorities agree that when a person is physically ill, the emotional state may be disturbed as well; similarly, the effect of the emotions on the health of the body is becoming more widely recognized in medical circles. The heart line reflects this balance and interplay between mind and body. A faint or shallow line suggests that the mental or emotional state is likely to upset the person's overall health, while a deeply colored or well-scored line suggests that physical problems are more likely to be the cause of poor health and, potentially, a depressed state of mind.

A palmar surface that is covered with a fine tracery of lines crisscrossing all over the place is a sure indication of a hypersensitive personality. The owner is fueled far too much by nervous energy, which he or she is unable to switch off. This, of course, saps the physical reserves, and eventually the subject's health is affected.

BELOW A clean, unmarked heart line is a sign of a good constitution – the subject is likely to enjoy a healthy, active life.

RIGHT A faint heart line indicates that the subject's health is likely to be affected by their emotional state. A deeply etched heart line, on the other hand, is a sign of poor physical state leading to depression.

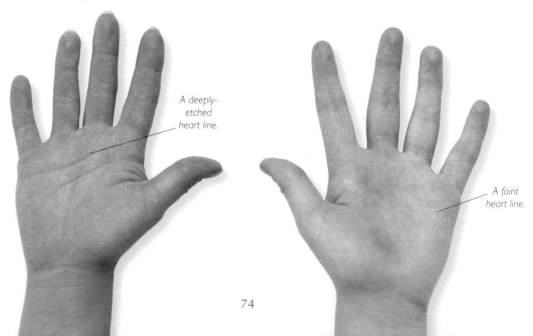

A deeply-etched heart line.

A faint heart line.

ISLANDS IN THE HEART LINE

An island at the start of the heart line, especially under the Saturn finger, implies a hearing defect, sometimes accompanied by balance problems which are caused by middle ear infections. In some cases there can also be a fear of heights or enclosed spaces. If this formation is found in both hands, this condition is accentuated. Make a quick check of the flexibility of the top phalange of the little finger. A supple or flexible tip assists better hearing in cases like these, while a stiff tip is very unhelpful.

An island on the line under the Apollo finger is associated with eye or sight defects. Traditionally, a circle or semicircle on the inside of the life line indicates the same thing. However, palmists generally agree that there is a definite correlation between the eyes and the heart line at this point.

A small series of three or four vertical lines just above the heart line and under the Mercury finger suggests dental weakness and teeth problems. Lighter marks imply gum disease, while heavy lines are said to refer to the teeth themselves.

Between the first and second points where deafness and sight problems are likely to be indicated, the line may chain, split, or form small islands. This is indicative of heart disease. Poor cardiovascular function, anxiety, a poor diet, or high blood pressure can be shown by an island in the heart line under the Mercury finger.

Please remember that, unless you are specifically trained, you cannot make a definite diagnosis of anything. If you find any of these indications on the palms of your subject, choose your words carefully when giving advice. By all means suggest a visit to the doctor for a checkup, but please weigh your words with great care. Diplomacy, sensitivity, and judgment are of paramount importance here.

BELOW Islands in the heart line may provide clues to the poor health of the subject.

islands in the heart line

THE FATE LINE

★ ★ ★ ★ ★ ★ ★ ★ ★ ★ ★ ★ ★ ★ ★ ★ ★ ★

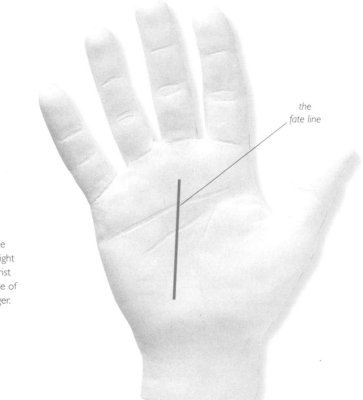

the fate line

RIGHT The fate line travels straight up from the wrist toward the base of the second finger.

Тhe line of fate is directly concerned with the way we see our path through life. It is a balance, a pivot, running straight up the hand from the wrist to the base of the middle finger – in extreme cases the line extends to the bottom phalange of the Saturn finger itself. The many forms and variations of this line have given rise to a whole host of different names for it: the line of awareness, career, destiny, environment, duty, or the Saturn line.

The line of fate governs the ambitions, but these are limited by the degree of faith the individual has in his or her own abilities. This line does not refer to material success or fame as such. Rather, it relates to the feeling of inner satisfaction at the results of our efforts to achieve personal aims. The lower down on the palm the line starts, the earlier those efforts begin.

It is rare to see the line properly formed on both hands, but those who do have a proper fate line on both left and right hands are individuals who are well balanced, aware of their responsibilities, and attuned to life. They move well in society and know how to approach people and tasks with equanimity.

A fate line on the left hand only suggests that the owner is full of dreams and aspirations but has little get-up-and-go to pursue them. When the line appears on the right hand only, the subject is generally quite appreciative of his or her lot in life but will make an effort to improve it.

When the fate line is absent, the subject will show little ambition, have poor social adaptability, and is likely to be inwardly unsettled. In the young especially, there is little sense of responsibility and virtually no pride in the self. Such a youngster needs to be carefully guided, otherwise he or she is likely to try all sorts of jobs that may last a few weeks at most. Such youngsters are often wasteful and disrespectful, unwilling to make more than the minimum effort if they're asked to do anything. This is accentuated if the palm is long, with short fingers. If the palm is soft to the touch and shorter than the fingers, or the middle finger is short and has a flexible tip, the owner will be an inherent gambler, someone who will take a chance rather than work a problem through properly.

The fate line proper can start from the wrist, inside the life line or just touching it. If it is inside the line of life it is really a duty line. Until it crosses the life line the owner will probably be pressured to follow family traditions in his or her choice of career – if the head of the family is a lawyer, for example, the son or daughter will also be expected to study law. For as long as this duty line remains inside the line of life, the youngster will have to do as he or she is told. Once the line passes out into the palm it may strengthen, take on a different direction, or fade away altogether. The individual can now choose whether or not to follow his or her own inclinations and ambitions. The stronger line suggests that he or she will continue to follow the family's wishes. A line moving in a different direction, a break, or any forking or branching implies some adaptation of the original idea that does not always work out to anyone's real satisfaction. When the line becomes weaker and fades away, the subject usually abandons family expectations and decides to pursue his or her own ambitions.

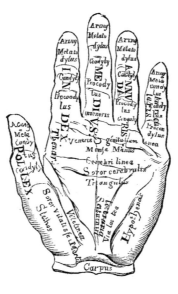

LEFT An early palmistry textual illustration showing the fate line and all the principal lines, giving the Latin names for the different areas of the palm.

BELOW When the line of fate is absent and the tip of the middle finger is flexible, you are probably looking at a gambler.

A fate line that starts at the life line suggests family support for the desired aim. For as long as the line stays close to the line of life, the family will back the subject all the way. Since this line can also indicate some sort of restriction, such as a health or financial matter that prevents complete autonomy, the owner will need to rely on this family support. Once the fate line moves away from the line of life, family support is either no longer needed or no longer available. The owner will now be confident enough and able to pursue his or her aims independently.

Regardless of where it originates, the higher on the palm the fate line starts, the

later in life the subject will develop enough determination or confidence to follow his or her ambition. The cause of this lack of confidence may have been a restrictive upbringing, or there may have been some other influence, equally difficult to shrug off. Once free, however, the subject will not be held back. In fact, late developers usually have a knack for success. They have borne disappointment for so long that they are not thrown by life's hard knocks. They just get up, dust themselves off, and keep trying and trying again until they succeed.

Sometimes this formation shows that the subject was unaware of his or her real

BELOW Are you seriously ambitious? Look for the loop of intent in the skin pattern below the middle and third finger.

CHERISHED AMBITIONS

Check between the bases of the middle and third fingers for a small loop in the skin pattern that enters the palmar surface and moves downward into the palm. This loop shows serious intent and marks a cherished ambition. It often begins as a simple hobby that develops over the years, until finally the subject is accepted as an authority in the particular area that has captivated him or her. When this pattern is found on both hands, this ambition will be a very serious matter indeed to the owner. No one will be allowed to get in the way – the owner will move heaven and earth to achieve the aim. The interest will be almost an obsession, right to the owner's dying day.

A clearly marked loop of intent.

RIGHT The loop of intent belongs to those who contemplate their ambitions constantly and never lose sight of their dreams.

*the line
of milieu*

ABOVE The line
of milieu may be
the mark of a late
developer.

potential. Such people may have been aware
of their interest, but not given the guidance
needed to pursue it. If this is the case, a weak
thumb or a low-set first and/or fourth finger
will aggravate the situation further.

If the line of fate begins on the Luna
mount and travels directly to the mount of
Saturn, without any significant interference
marks, the subject will have sufficient
confidence in his or her abilities to brook no
opposition. Often people with this
formation want a career that requires public
approval, such as entertainment, politics, or
some other form of public life. Pursuing any
work that depends on public acceptance for
its success shows extreme faith in one's own
abilities and potential.

Occasionally a line appears between the
life line and the main fate line: this is called
the line of milieu. It suggests problems for

as long as it is present on a hand, preventing
the individual from following his or her
ambitions. It may be family
difficulties, financial dilemmas,
health problems, or some other
obstacle that, for one reason or
another, the subject is unable to
overcome. But as soon as the line stops,
whatever is causing the restriction comes to
an end too. Any small influence line between
the fate line and the milieu line aggravates
the situation.

If there are many small milieu lines, they
will influence the subject, but the more there
are the less their obstructive value. They are
more likely to represent the petty trials and
tribulations that we all experience from time
to time but can't do much about – life's
ordinary little hiccups that have to be taken
in our strides.

BELOW
Entertainers and
public figures tend
to have a clear line
of fate that starts
on the Luna mount
and then travels
directly to the
mount of Saturn.

Inclinations from the Line of Fate

✦ ✦ ✦ ✦ ✦ ✦ ✦ ✦ ✦ ✦ ✦ ✦ ✦ ✦

WHEN A LINE of fate starts from more than one source it suggests as many interests as there are sources. Sometimes these different sources may also indicate a conflict of interests. For example, a branch that originates from the mount of Venus and merges with a line from the Luna mount implies that family interests probably conflict with personal aims. The stronger line will show the direction the subject's career will eventually take.

One line may start from the wrist, the mount of Neptune, or just a little higher on the hand and merge with a fork coming from the Luna mount. Such a line formation was traditionally thought to imply a long and happy marriage. Now, however, it is viewed somewhat differently – it is thought to indicate one of those very special close friendships with someone we can always count on for support.

RIGHT A long and lasting marriage is traditionally said to be denoted by a fork coming from the Luna mount which merges with one from the mount of Neptune.

RIGHT Any fork in the fate line suggests fame, fortune, or both. Those who left their marks on Hollywood Boulevard might have this kind of formation.

The fate line's usual path is to the Saturn mount, but it can move in any direction and end anywhere in the palm. A line that ends on the Jupiter mount suggests very strong ambitions and high motivation for personal achievement and success, with a correspondingly strong belief in oneself. This may manifest itself in a desire to interact with others and to teach or instruct in some way, or in a willingness to seek or take public office.

A line that stops on the Apollo mount indicates natural creative talents. However, this is more the area of the Apollo line, which we will deal with elsewhere.

Any fork in the fate line can suggest fame, fortune, or both. A fork between Jupiter and Apollo implies the sort of high-profile career associated with power and influence. With Mercury, it may be natural commercial expertise. Branches shared by Saturn and Mercury could indicate a gift for medical research. A branch between Jupiter and Saturn could indicate a legal career culminating on the bench as a judge. A branch between Jupiter and Mercury suggests a career in money, either banking or the stock market. A branch between Saturn and Apollo often appears on the hands of comedians.

When the line of fate merges with or stops at the heart line, an emotional decision will be made that may negatively influence the subject's career and ambitions. Any

influence lines from elsewhere may indicate a scandal or similar difficulty. If the line has forked just prior to this, note where this other prong originates, for that will indicate the source of the trouble.

A fork actually on the heart line shows an instinctive mind, someone who knows how to weigh the factors and make the right decision at the right time to achieve advantage and success. Along with this decision may come a diversification of interests, which shows that the owner is also ready to take on more responsibility.

A fork between the heart and head lines shows changes that the subject has made to his or her life. The reasons for these changes will be indicated by the proximity of the fork to either the head or heart line. If it is nearer the heart line, for example, an instinctive matter is implied, a situation in which the owner "just knows" the right thing to do. A fork nearer the head line indicates more practical reasons for the change, perhaps caused by unforeseen external circumstances. The subject in this case has a more materialistic outlook.

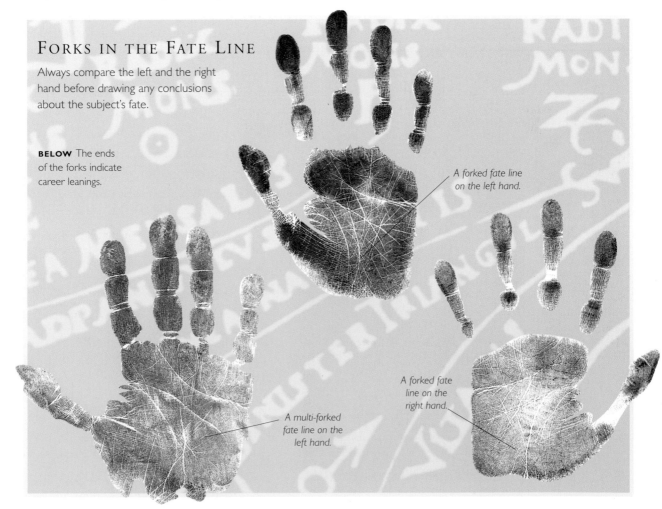

FORKS IN THE FATE LINE

Always compare the left and the right hand before drawing any conclusions about the subject's fate.

BELOW The ends of the forks indicate career leanings.

A forked fate line on the left hand.

A forked fate line on the right hand.

A multi-forked fate line on the left hand.

A firm line of fate, with few or no breaks or influence marks, indicates a resolute character, someone who will take most things in their stride. If the line weakens or tails off, whatever success has been achieved may come to an end.

A line of fate that is made up of many different strands from all over the place shows that the owner has an indecisive nature, the sort of person who tries this and that but actually gets nowhere in the end. There is a definite lack of sustained drive and initiative in this person.

There may be one or a series of influence lines coming from the outer edge of the hand to join the line of fate. If there are more than one, note how many. The more there are, the more sensitive the owner. These folks fare better in a partnership, for then they don't have to be so self-reliant. The strongest influence line shows who is dominant in the relationship.

An influence line that starts with an island heralds trouble. The difficulty may be only temporary, but this sort of line indicates that the subject shouldn't place too much trust in this influence. If this little line is very strongly marked, this other person will be a very strong influence, quite possibly the dominant partner of the two.

If such a line goes directly to the base of the Saturn finger to merge with the rarely seen Ring of Saturn, a single-minded ambition will override all other plans and considerations. Nothing will be allowed to get in the way of this person's desire and dream for success.

NAPOLEON'S FATE

The long, straight, direct line of fate suggests a very strong sense of duty, possibly misplaced. With this mark comes a feeling of some inescapable destiny or duty that cannot be changed. It is widely suspected by palmists that Napoleon had this sort of line on both hands.

RIGHT It has been suggested that Napoleon's line of fate on both palms was long and straight, denoting an unwavering sense of destiny.

FAR RIGHT A long prominent fate line is an indication of a resolute character.

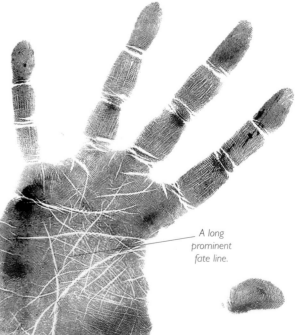

A long prominent fate line.

THE LIFE-SAVING CROSS

There is one other special mark concerned with the line of fate. About an inch and a half (three to four centimeters) up from the base of the hand, there may be a small cross between the lines of life and fate. If this cross touches both lines, it is known as the life-saving cross, and it denotes someone whose career involves helping or caring for others.

The life-saving cross is found on the hands of those people like doctors, nurses, coastguards, and paramedics. If the cross is absent entirely, there may be a trace of bitterness in the overall character.

BELOW The life-saving cross is a mark found on the palms of healers and carers such as Florence Nightingale.

RIGHT The life-saving cross appears between the lines of fate and life.

the life-saving cross

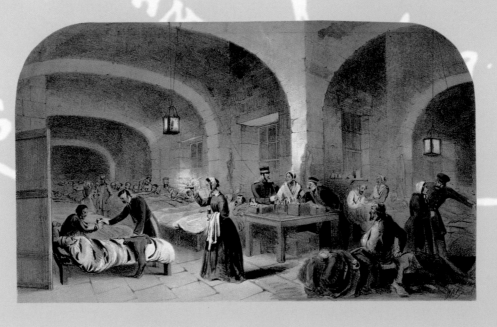

PART THREE

THE MINOR LINES AND OTHER FEATURES

★ ★ ★ ★ ★

Reading a hand is a bit like putting together a jigsaw puzzle – once we have the outline, we can fill in the details. Trying to distinguish them all can be like walking in a minefield. It is so easy to give too much credence to one mark, and not enough thought to another.

The term "minor" is something of a misnomer, for all lines have equal importance in hand analysis. These lesser lines help hone the implications of the principal lines, for the extra information they provide fills out the real character and personality.

There are more likely to be minor lines and other features on a conic hand. But wherever they are found they give their contribution to the overall assessment.

There is no particular significance to the order in which these lesser lines are discussed here, although some of them are slightly more influential. For accuracy it is always crucial to compare the left and right hand before coming to a conclusion.

ABOVE The minor lines of the hand are just as important as the principal lines, since they reveal further detailed clues to the subject's personality.

THE SUN LINES

★ ★ ★ ★ ★ ★ ★ ★ ★ ★ ★ ★ ★ ★ ★ ★ ★ ★

A Sun line, sister line to the fate line.

RIGHT The Sun line, or line of Apollo, confers happiness. It can be found on most hands in some shape or form.

T HE SUN, OR Apollo, line is a sister line to the fate line. It is often mistaken for the Mercury or health line. If both lines are present there is not much of a problem, but if only one line is found, be aware that it is not always obvious which it is.

This line is found in some form on many hands. Tradition has it that it confers brilliance, riches, fame, and success. In my experience, however, this is not so. Nor is the line a guarantee of inner happiness, although when it is present, the owner can usually be assumed to be a basically happy person. While the subject may reap material rewards from whatever talents are indicated, it is really inner happiness that this line refers to.

Whenever it is found, no matter what the formation of the hand, the owner will have talent and a capacity for hard work. Such people are really only happy when they are stretched to the limit. No matter what their individual talent may be, these people earn respect for their abilities.

When the Sun line begins at the wrist and goes straight to the mount of Apollo, it theoretically indicates a long and happy life

that may end with social distinction and wealth. However, the subject has to work hard to achieve these benefits – they are not conferred on him or her as a matter of course. A short, segmented, or otherwise partially formed Sun line may indicate a five-minute wonder.

As a rule this line begins either at the head line or between the head line and the heart line. It can also start actually on the line of heart, or just after it. It can start with a fork and may end in one, or in the traditional trident formation.

Should the line begin inside the line of life or on the mount of Venus, the family will be helpful throughout the subject's life. Should the line touch or begin just away from the line of life, influential people will always be there to support and assist the subject when needed.

If the line starts on the mount of Neptune, the owner will have a special gift for dealing with people.

If the line starts anywhere on the mount of the Moon, the owner will enjoy a life of prominence, one that relies on very hard

ABOVE In Tarot the sun symbolizes growth, happiness, generosity, and prosperity.

work not only to remain in the public eye, but at the top of their professional ladder.

The later the Sun line starts – that is, the further up the palm from the wrist – the greater the subject's innate talent and persistence in achieving his or her ambitions. This is particularly true if the Sun line begins in the zone of Mars. A Sun line that starts here usually suggests a public life in community work or politics.

If the line has a forked start, especially in the zone of Mars, the subject is likely to have more than one string to his or her bow and may follow two or even more careers. If the subject practices two professions, one may well be the opposite of the other. A close examination of the branches should indicate which is the more favored of these two lives.

When the line of Sun starts from the head line it indicates that extra little bit of determination brought about by the desire to succeed. Late starters often have more success than those who began earlier.

A Sun line that ends at the head line suggests disaster. Whatever the situation, the subject never really recovers.

A Sun line that starts from the line of heart implies emotional overtones to the subject's ambitions. A line that ends here may indicate destruction of everything meaningful to the subject, not only material possessions, but prestige or honor as well.

When the line of Sun starts above the line of heart, the subject's goals are a labor of love, and probably little help is given from outside sources. However, these people usually don't need much help. They are self-reliant, directed, and determined.

The success line that begins from the Luna mount suggests change brought about by circumstances over which the subject has little or no control. It may be an unforeseen lucky win, or an unexpected inheritance.

Sometimes the line of fate meets and merges with the Sun line. When this happens, all of the owner's ambitions will be realized. When the fate and Sun lines appear together, look to see which one is the stronger. A stronger Sun line indicates an uninhibited and outgoing personality. A stronger fate line, however, indicates the more serious character whose personality is not as sunny. An influence line between them shows help from an influential source.

A marriage line, or an influence line from a marriage line, shows a liaison that will end in disgrace. If the influence line is islanded, expect a scandal attached to the relationship.

To have a positive effect, the Sun line must be free of restricting influence lines throughout its course. Even good influence marks have negative effects on this line.

A hand without any trace of a Sun line shows an inability to understand personal limitations. Such people will take all sorts of chances and believe in their own publicity. They feel immune from harm.

Occasionally, although rarely, there may be a collection of several Sun lines. This shows talent and versatility in several fields.

BELOW A palm showing a clear Sun line on the Apollo mount. A long Sun line promises happiness and success during your lifetime!

A Sun line going toward the Apollo mount.

THE MERCURY LINE

* * * * * * * * * * * * * * * *

RIGHT The line of Mercury has a variety of names: the line of health, or the Hepatica, liver, stomach or business line. The presence of this line is not usually beneficial.

the Mercury line

BELOW A Mercury line that starts in the zone of Mars (the god of war, shown below) is likely to belong to a business-minded individual.

RIGHT A Mercury line may denote the kind of person who is obsessed with taking pills.

Tʜᴇ ʟɪɴᴇ ᴏf Mercury, also known variously as the health line or the Hepatica, liver, stomach, or business line, is sometimes mistaken for the line of intuition (see page 98). While it is easy to see how they may be mistaken one for the other, they have very different implications. It is better for this line not to be present in the hand. If it is found, there will almost certainly be some sort of physical weakness, possibly lasting or recurring. The subject will be particularly concerned with diet and well-being, hygiene matters, and fitness, often to the extent of becoming a hypochondriac.

The line usually travels from somewhere near the life line, directly from the line itself, or even from inside the life line, and runs toward the mount of Mercury. Sometimes it begins on the Luna mount. It can be badly fragmented or a wholesome, well-etched marking from start to end.

When it starts on the mount of Venus and, therefore, inside the line of life, it denotes a natural worrier, digestive weakness, and a predisposition to either avoid or regularly take supplementary remedies, vitamins and minerals. If the allergy line is present (see page 101), the owner may have a real or imagined allergy; this is the type of person for whom placebos were invented. In extreme cases, this person may talk as if he or she has had every illness and health problem under the sun. When the line starts from the life line itself there will be an aversion to taking pills, even just to ease everyday aches and pains such as a simple headache.

Only when this line starts in the central area of the palm, away from the line of life, do all these behavioral traits lessen somewhat; in this case the subject usually has a trouble-free health life.

A Mercury line that begins in the zone of Mars is actually a business-orientated line. Commerce and business are the focal point of the subject's interests, and the subject shows a natural aptitude for high finance. In some cases this is a sign of the natural salesman, someone able to read trends and seize the opportunities they present.

When the Mercury line crosses the path of the head line, there may also be influence lines from one to the other. If these occur in both hands, there will be an interest in occult matters. If the line fragments as it crosses the head line, the subject will have varying interests. Several fragments crossing the head line low on the Luna mount indicate an extremely fertile imagination.

If the head line is forked and the Mercury line crosses both branches, expect to find hypersensitivity and a worrying mind that is rarely still. On an "empty" hand this may not be too much of a problem, but on a "full" hand it will lead to poor health because of too much nervous energy being used without adequate rest.

the Mercury line

A Mercury line that starts at the head line refers to business activity that is somewhat less instinctive. When the line crosses the heart line and touches any of the small vertical lines on the mount of Mercury, there will be interest in healing.

Recently it has been suggested that a long, straight Mercury line can imply a sense of self-delusion or social inhibition brought about by introversion. If the first and fourth fingers are very low-set, or the thumb appears too weak for the hand, this may be the case.

ABOVE A square hand showing a Mercury line. If the line begins in the center of the palm the subject will have few health problems.

LEFT Ideally, if you do have a Mercury line, it will start in the zone of Mars, denoting a head for business.

THE SIMIAN LINE

* * * * * * * * * * * * * * * * *

the simian line

STRICTLY SPEAKING, THE simian line is a fusion of the line of head with the line of heart. It is found on all kinds of people. It frequently appears on the hands of obsessive people who feel driven to succeed and will not be diverted from their goal. They must achieve despite their circumstances. These people channel all their energy into a well-orchestrated attack on the subject matter at hand.

Many intelligent and articulate people have this marking, but they rarely direct their talents as well as they should. Such a character trait may manifest itself in several different ways. For one thing, these people may seem different from everyone else in everything they do. There is an air of control, they have to be right, they deal in facts, not probabilities or possibilities. If something isn't right, it's wrong! Such people are sometimes good leaders, but they will dispense with niceties to achieve their aims.

They don't expect to be popular, and they can be hard taskmasters if that's what it takes to get a job done.

The head line governs intellect and perception, while the heart line controls emotional response. One without the other, or one weaker than the other, will upset this delicate balance. The space between the head and heart lines indicates the ability to reason and think with a certain amount of detachment. A reasonable amount of space here indicates objectivity and common sense. The narrower the space, however, the more emotions come into play, and when the two lines fuse completely there is an increased intensity of purpose, and any imbalance between intellect and emotions is more readily observable.

The above applies when the simian line is set low on the palm, which is often the case. Occasionally, however, the line is set high, indicating that intellect or reason is more dominant. If the line is thicker at the start, near the thumb side of the hand, the subject

ABOVE The simian line denotes someone like Martin Luther King, who was passionate about causes and did not tolerate resistance; they are often inspirational orators.

will have a colder and more calculating emotional style. When the line is thicker at the outer edge of the palm, emotions are instinctive. A thick line straight across the palm is a sure sign of a selfish and materialistic nature.

A thin line straight across the palm is rare, but when present it indicates a hypersensitive mentality, with excellent perception – the sort of person who can answer a question before the other person's asked it. However, the principal motivation of these people is self-interest. Egocentric, they often think they are infallible and are ruthless toward opposition of any kind. They will sacrifice anything and anyone to attain their ends, and often act like overgrown children when they aren't allowed to have their own way. They cannot sit still for long and have to keep their hands and mind occupied. It is characteristic of these people to love and hate with equal intensity – there are no half measures.

A simian line – the head and heart line are fused.

When the simian line appears on the left hand only, the owner may have a tendency to work in fits and starts, giving their all one day and nothing the next. When it's found on the right hand only, expect to find a Jekyll and Hyde personality. In this case, however, the subject is always fully conscious of his or her actions and their effect on others.

People with simian lines love gadgets and anything that is new-fangled. They are often very enthusiastic and may become efficient collectors, pursuing their hobby with the same intensity that they apply to everything else.

Most of the time, there is little to indicate that these people are any different from the rest of us. Only when they are goaded into action do all these extremes of behavior surface and their true colors show through.

THE RASCETTES

* * * * * * * * * * * * * * * * *

the rascettes

THE RASCETTES, OR bracelets, are the lines that run across the inside of the wrist at the base of the palm. Usually there are one, two, or three of these lines, but there may be even more. Eastern palmistry gives them far more significance than Western schools of thought.

Traditionally these lines are said to be linked with longevity, but practice does not support this theory. However, they have appeared on the hands of several people who have lived well into their nineties and beyond, and a few centenarians had life lines that reached down and touched or even passed through the first wrist line!

If a woman's first bracelet arches or rises into the base of the palm, it suggests difficulties with the genitourinal system, anything from bladder problems to menstrual difficulties. It makes sense to look at the hands of young girls to see whether this formation is present. If it is, any problems that arise could, through judicial intervention and treatment, save some embarrassment in adolescence and perhaps avoid any complications later on. If, in later years, the reproductive system is upset – if, for example, a hysterectomy is needed – it may be reflected in the top rascette, which will have started to arch upward into the base of the palm.

If the second rascette also arches into the palm, the weaknesses implied by the first arch will be aggravated. In such circumstances, any third line present will usually be badly formed, chained, or weak-looking, and will just make things worse. This upward arching of the bracelets is sometimes seen in men, where it may reflect prostate or similar problems.

It is preferable for the rascettes to pass straight across the wrist in firm lines; in fact, three well-formed lines crossing the wrist together are known in palmistry as the "magic bracelet." In Eastern palmistry this is said to confer special good luck, rather like having your own personal built-in charm bracelet. It is believed in some quarters that those with this particular formation are immune to travel sickness.

TRAVEL AND THE BRACELETS

The bracelets are also said to relate to certain travel matters. A line from the top wrist line to the Jupiter mount suggests fame and fortune connected with foreign travel. An influence line to the Saturn mount, however, suggests serious problems while traveling abroad.

An influence line to the mount of Apollo suggests a fame that is more far-reaching abroad than it is at home. If such a line reaches the Mercury mount, it means great business success in foreign countries. In Japanese, Chinese, and Indian palmistry this is thought to be a fairly rare influence line, but if it is present it is said to confer sudden wealth.

Any influence line from one of the bracelets that goes to anywhere on the Luna mount indicates a great love of travel in any form. The more lines there are, the more the subject is likely to indulge this love. Often, though, he or she enjoys traveling more for the stimulation that it provides than for the actual journey itself.

Travel-related issues may also be reflected elsewhere on the hand. For example, a number of fine lines are sometimes seen going from percussion edge to the Luna mount, under the head line. If these lines are well formed, with no breaks or interference marks of any kind, then journeys may be safely made. If one of these lines turns downward at its end, the journey will end in problems, or problems will occur because of it. If the line sends a small influence mark upward or turns upward itself, then the journey will more than likely have a successful and happy conclusion.

If the influence is traced to the Jupiter mount, the owner can expect success in anything to do with personal ambitions or social prestige through travel. A line to the mount of Saturn suggests the scientific area, while a line to the Apollo mount implies success in the creative arts. An influence line to the mount of Mercury suggests business or career matters.

A square on any of these small influence marks gives protection during a journey. An island usually hints at trouble, but a star at the end of a line promises a brilliant finale to any travel-related enterprise. A circle on or near any travel line, especially at the end of the line, is a traditional sign of danger connected with travel by water. I include air travel when I see this mark.

ABOVE A line from one of the bracelets to the Luna mount indicates the desire to travel.

A bracelet rising toward the base of the palm.

ABOVE Should the bracelet on a female subject rise to the base of the palm, look out for problems in the reproductive system in later years.

RIGHT An influence line from the rascettes to the Luna mount denotes a great love of travel.

Influence lines from the bracelet to the Luna mount.

FRUSTRATION LINES

Sometimes restlessness and frustration can be mistaken for one another. To make the distinction, it helps to look for a small series of vertical lines at the basal phalanges of the fingers. These lines, regardless of their individual formation or the hand type on which they are found, are a sure sign of frustration, which can manifest itself as restlessness and the need for change.

The finger on which the lines appear indicates the area of difficulty. If they are at the base of the Jupiter finger, the subject may have a problem with religious convictions, or may be unable to achieve his or her ambitions or a better social standing. On the middle finger, the lines indicate difficulty in relationships. If the lines appear on the third finger, there may be problems connected with the creative arts. Frustration lines on the little finger indicate difficulties in career, communications, or business affairs. When the lines occur on all the fingers, all these indications may be enhanced, and there will be an overall inability to cope with stress. Any sudden reversals completely throw this type of person off course.

SISTER LINES

All major and minor lines can have a double, or sister line, that follows the same course as the principal line for a part of the way, or fades and returns a little later.

When the major line shows an obvious weakness, the sister line acts as a backup, providing assistance for as long as it is needed. If there is no sign of weakness, the sister line may be showing an alternative attitude or way of life to that indicated by the principal line. This is often the case when the sister line runs almost the entire course of the line it supports. It indicates that two entirely different lives may be pursued by the subject at the same time.

RIGHT Depending on which finger the frustration lines appear, different difficulties will be registered.

Lines on the Saturn finger – relationship problems.

Lines on the Jupiter finger – difficulties connected with ambition or religion.

Lines on the Apollo finger – problems connected with creativity.

Lines on the Mercury finger – money problems.

STRESS, STRAIN, AND RESTLESSNESS

A purely restless soul is indicated by a series of very fine small lines that enter the palm from the percussion just above the head line. This signifies a dislike of physical inactivity. These people are compulsive – they have to be doing something. Wide spaces between the fingers add to the restlessness. People's hands may show stress and strain in several different ways. Most often, it is suggested by a fluffy appearance to the head line. If the strain gets unbearable it may affect the person's physical state, in which case the life line may also fluff up. Emotional stress is shown by a similar appearance to the heart line.

stress or strain lines

Small horizontal white lines across the top phalanges of any of the fingers suggest physical stress and strain. This is often seen on the hands of those who insist on burning the candle at both ends for too long. Called simply "white lines," they can be quite temporary and appear overnight or, more usually, over the day, for they are most likely to appear at the end of a particularly

trying time. If the subject hasn't taken time for adequate food, drink, or rest, the physical and nervous energy reserves will be depleted. After a meal and a good night's sleep, the lines will usually disappear.

More permanent stress and strain will be emphasized by a badly formed Girdle of Venus or *Via Lascivia* (see pages 99–101). Should this be accompanied by white flecks in the nails, especially if those nails are bitten, the whole nervous system will be in very bad shape. These signs are nature's way of telling the subject to slow down. Should the warnings be ignored, the owner's physical weak spots will give way. If this happens, the time needed to restore his or her health may be long, painful, and costly in more ways than one.

LEFT Any stress or strain you may have undergone will show up in a "fluffy" head line.

LEFT A stressful occupation may be unavoidable in the modern world. It will show in fine lines entering the palm from the percussion side of the palm above the head line.

LEFT Small, white horizontal lines across the top of the nail suggest stress and strain.

RINGS AND OTHER
NOTABLE FEATURES

* * * * * * * * * * * * * * * * * *

THE FAMILY RING

This is really the line that separates the second phalange of the thumb from the top of mount of Venus. This is the only "ring" as such that does not look like a ring. It is not a line that has a cutting-off effect; as a rule it is chained or fragmented, lightly marked in some hands but quite strong and noticeable in others.

If there is not a great deal of affection for the other members of the family, the ring will be almost nonexistent. However, a strongly etched ring reveals that the subject has a close family relationship.

A ring that seems more heavily marked at the top inner side of the thumb but weaker at the lower end suggests that, as in many families, things were fine once, but the good feelings seem to have petered out over time.

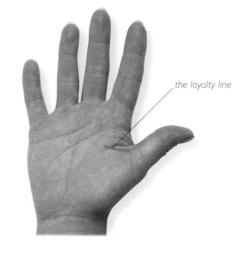

the loyalty line

the family ring

ABOVE The family ring, between the thumb and the Venus mount, will reveal a great deal about your family relationships.

THE LOYALTY LINE

Sometimes a line or a small collection of lines, originating near the family ring and reaching to the life line, appear across the top of the mount of Venus. This formation indicates a sense of loyalty to or a constant need for a particular family member or members. Should the line actually start at the family ring, this will be enhanced. If there is more than one line and they all begin here, the family will be so close-knit that almost no one will be allowed to penetrate it. The subject's uppermost thoughts will be for the good name of the family in which he or she was raised.

Any influence lines that stay within the life line show problems contained entirely within the family circle.

THE RING OF SOLOMON

Also known as the Jupiter ring, this line crosses along the top of the mount of Jupiter (not around the base of the finger, as suggested by older writers). It is believed to confer an air of authority and the ability to teach others.

the ring of Solomon

A well-formed ring of Solomon indicates personal honor, social position, integrity, and prestige. Some owners of this line may take up important positions of public responsibility by taking on roles such as magistrate or local politician. However, a poorly formed or fragmented marking

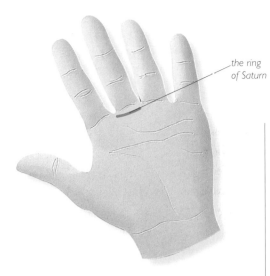

*the ring
of Saturn*

suggests a person who may enter into shady dealings and may even find themselves on the wrong side of the law.

THE RING OF SATURN

This is an unfortunate marking, usually a small broken line that circles the base of the middle finger along the top of the mount. This subject lacks spontaneity, flexibility, and social graces. He or she is very much a loner and prefers it that way. It is extremely difficult to persuade such people to get out and about socially, and probably not worth the effort – they really are best left to their own devices.

THE RING OF APOLLO

There are two meanings associated with this rather rare marking, which encircles the base of the third finger on the top of the Apollo mount. A well-made ring confers special accomplishment in public life,

*the ring
of Apollo*

in areas such as entertainment, or the arts. Really special personalities, who clearly stand out head and shoulders above their contemporaries have this ring.

A word of caution, however. When this mark appears on both hands, it often signifies a fall from grace, or a slipping from an exalted position in the public eye.

A poorly formed ring of Apollo indicates someone with poor taste and bad judgment. No matter how hard they struggle to impress, these people just don't seem able to get anything quite right.

THE RING OF MERCURY

An extremely rare pattern, this ring encircles the base of the fourth finger, often in broken form. Traditionally, it is said to be the true mark of the confirmed bachelor or spinster. There is little or no desire in this person to participate in an intimate relationship with a member of the opposite sex. In fact, though (quite contrary to popular belief), these people do get along well with the opposite sex and are not necessarily homosexual.

In a more material sense this line will, on a firm hand, confer business acumen and a drive to achieve wealth and power. Such people will put aside all other considerations to pursue these goals. However, a poorly formed ring suggests someone who is involved in truly questionable financial activities.

*the ring of
Mercury*

BELOW The ring of Saturn usually denotes a loner who is best left to his or her own devices.

RIGHT
Conventional
physicians or
alternative healers
are likely to have
the medical
stigmata.

THE MEDICAL STIGMATA

This is a series of three, four, or even five small vertical lines slightly to the inner side of the Mercury finger and just above the heart line. Owners of these lines have an aptitude for medicine, whether conventional or alternative, and tend to concentrate particularly on healing. Sometimes these lines can reflect dental problems. There is a another school of thought that claims they can appear in a mild form of hypochondria.

THE LINE OF INTUITION

This is a small semicircular line that may begin anywhere on the percussion edge of the Luna mount, arc into the palm, and turn upward to end on the mount of Mercury. Usually this line is fragmented into islands, chains, or what looks like a collection of seemingly small, unconnected influence lines. However, in the rare instances when an unbroken line appears, the subject will almost certainly have an investigative mind and an excellent memory. Owners of a line of intuition are often widely read and well

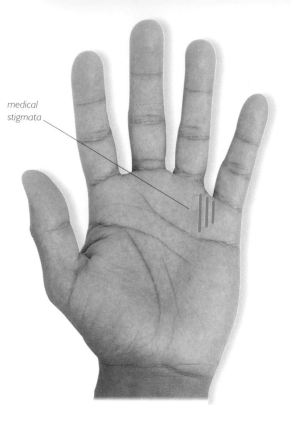

medical
stigmata

educated, and able to express themselves with fluency and clarity. They often find that they instinctively "just know" things without really understanding why.

Because of their innate prescience, many of these folks drift into the occult. Some are natural mediums, or able to quickly learn the ancient but more practical arts of prediction. They may also have some fundamental hypnotic ability, which they may use in their work. This will be especially true if the line ends on the mount of Mars positive. A line of intuition that forms a triangle in combination with the fate line and the head line is traditionally thought to enhance these powers with the gift of prophecy.

The more faults the line has, the weaker these powers will be. If the line is very wavy, fragmented, frayed, or islanded, any innate prescience is weak, spasmodic, and not always to be relied upon.

If there is a line of intuition on an elementary hand, no matter what the line's formation is, the subject will be completely in harmony with nature.

BELOW The line of
intuition is likely to
be found on the
hands of those who
instinctively "know"
without really
recognizing why.

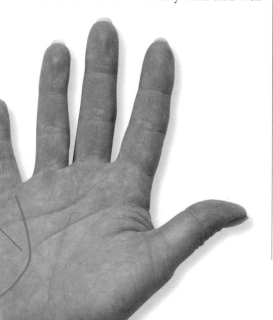

the line
of intuition

THE GIRDLE OF VENUS AND THE *VIA LASCIVIA*

Two of the lesser or minor lines have a combined effect that can be quite devastating if their mutual energies are misused or not fully understood by the subject. The first of these, called the Girdle of Venus, is a small semicircular line that is found between the base of the fingers and the heart line. The other line, known as the *Via Lascivia*, is a small horizontal or semicircular line that usually links the base of the Luna and Venus mounts.

These are two of the most misunderstood and misinterpreted features of the hand. Each is concerned with sensitivity – the Girdle refers to emotional sensitivity, while the *Via Lascivia* relates to the physical side. They may both appear on the hand or be found separately, either on one hand or the other. Strictly speaking, they have nothing at all to do with each other, but in fact they share an uncanny affinity in that they both relate to excessive behavior.

LEFT Cardinal Chigi heals plague-ridden Romans in this 17th-century painting. People with a line of intuition may be associated with the occult and may use their powers to benefit others.

BELOW To become another Sherlock Holmes you would benefit from a line of intuition; if the line is unbroken you are bound to have a thorough investigative mind.

the Girdle of Venus

LEFT The Girdle of Venus denotes emotional sensitivity and even inner turmoil.

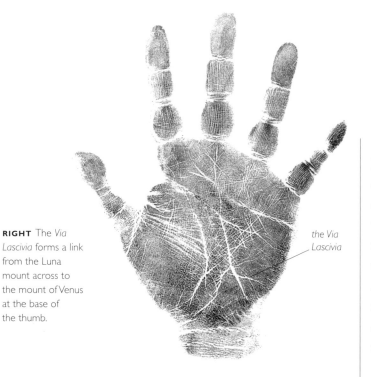

RIGHT The *Via Lascivia* forms a link from the Luna mount across to the mount of Venus at the base of the thumb.

the Via Lascivia

The Girdle of Venus lies along the top of the hand as either a firm line between the fourth mount and the first finger base, or as a series of badly fragmented markings. It may be chained or frayed, islanded, or tasselated, and it can be either long or short. Whatever the formation, the fact that it is there at all indicates sensitivity in the owner's emotional outlook, because of the Girdle's location – along the top of the emotional part of the hand near the heart line.

A straightforward line without any breaks or other faults suggests inner emotional turmoil. This type is not consistent in his or her approach to romance, sex, or relationships. There is a healthy outlook, and the subject has a very responsive nature, but he or she may be indiscreet or too flirtatious. When these people are "up" they are full of enthusiasm and spirited, sometimes reaching dizzying heights of euphoria. But when they are "down," they fall so low it seems nothing will drag them up from the mire.

ABOVE Those who have a Girdle of Venus have a healthy appearance but may be flirtatious or indiscreet.

When the Girdle is found on a conic hand, the subject craves constant stimulation of the senses. If found on a square hand, the owner will succumb to extreme nervousness the moment anyone takes him or her to task for a word or deed, no matter how innocent that word or deed may have originally been. A Girdle on a spatulate hand will cause nervous excitability. This subject is never still and is always on the lookout for something new to play or fiddle with.

A Girdle on a knotty hand indicates someone inclined to let go of all control as a demanding task reaches its successful conclusion. On a mixed hand, excitability and high nervous tension are marked. These people cannot keep a secret as they wait for their "moment" to divulge the news. Sometimes there is also a gambling streak in this subject type.

A Girdle of Venus on an elementary hand is almost a contradiction in terms. However, it has been known to happen occasionally, and when it does, the owner will have a very low boiling point. Provoke this person at your peril!

Generally, the line is composed of fragments and bits and pieces, suggesting a less intense emotional outlook. The shorter the line from the Saturn mount to the Apollo or Jupiter mounts, the more controlled the subject's responses. A short line from the Saturn mount to the Apollo or Mercury mounts indicates a more instinctive outlook, but the subject's sensitivity is near the surface. A poor line indicates more practicality with healthier emotional responses – common sense usually prevails.

A double or triple Girdle is not good at all. The owner actively seeks sensory stimulation and will stop at nothing to get it. He or she will freely experiment with sex, alcohol, and drugs. Badly formed double or triple Girdles only make things worse and in extreme cases may even lead to crime.

Perhaps the only time the Girdle serves a useful purpose is when it is found on a hand with sensitivity pads on the inner side of the top phalanges of the fingers and thumbs. These indicate that the subject's esthetic qualities are brought into play. The senses are heightened and natural abilities are more refined, and there is an appreciation of the arts. There is often intense fastidiousness.

The presence of the *Via Lascivia*, usually a small semicircular line linking the Venus and Luna mounts, indicates a strong need for physical stimulation or excitement. Like the Girdle, it can be short or long and may be badly broken or fragmented, tasselated, frayed, chained, or islanded. It may be present on one hand or both.

When the line simply links the two mounts, it indicates a constant need for physical stimulation to counteract boredom. The subject will try anything once. If the line starts from the Venus mount and curves and twists its way to the Luna mount, excesses in such activity will be considered par for the course.

The owner of a *Via Lascivia* on a soft square or round hand will do almost anything to pursue his or her desires, although the square-handed person is likely to show a little more common sense than one with a round hand.

The straighter the line, the more it may act as an allergy line. In medieval times this was referred to as the poison line, because very little was known about allergies in those days; if someone died after eating or drinking something, it was assumed that he or she had been poisoned. Today we understand that people with this line may be hypersensitive to particular foods, drinks, or drugs, or they may simply have an aversion to certain substances.

When the *Via Lascivia* and the Girdle of Venus appear together, there is a danger of excessive behavior, although if the hand is firm to the touch and the head line is short and well formed, temptations to overindulge are generally kept under control. However, on a soft hand, with a long head line or overdeveloped mounts of Venus and Luna, life won't exactly be dull. The owner will live life to the full, but is likely to succumb to a surfeit of excesses sooner rather than later.

ABOVE The presence of the *Via Lascivia* indicates someone who will go to any ends to fulfill their physical needs – this subject could succumb to gluttony.

THE DISTINCTIVE MINOR MARKS

* * * * * * * * * * * * * * * * *

THE SPECIAL MARKS discussed in this chapter may be found anywhere on the hand, not just on the palm but also on the sides or back of the hand, and, of course, intermingled with the lines. They have group as well as individual interpretations, although the meanings are subject to change depending on where the lines are found. The meanings given here are those used in Western hand analysis.

The minor marks are the bar, chain, circle, cross, dot, grille, island, square, star, tassel, triangle, trident, and the single vertical line. Each of these may appear on its own, in conjunction with a line or other marks, or it may be accidentally created as a result of the meeting of any major or minor lines.

For practical purposes we can say that the circle, square, star, triangle, trident, and vertical line, which usually appear on the mounts, generally have positive attributes. The other marks – the bar, chain, cross, dot, grille, island, and tassel – tend to have a negative effect wherever they are located. Any mark that appears on a line or is formed accidentally can easily take on another meaning according to where it is found. If a mark is found on a mount it could mean one thing, but an identical mark on a line on that mount, could have a different meaning.

ABOVE Minor marks on the hand may indicate significant events in your life. A circle on the Jupiter mount indicates academic success.

THE BAR

Any obstruction on a line weakens the effect of that line by stopping the flow of energy. As a rule, a bar indicates a delay in the subject's plans. If the line is weaker after the barring, whatever event or difficulty the bar represents has left its mark on the individual.

THE CHAIN

A chain, which looks like a series of small connected islands, also has a weakening effect on a line. When seen on the life line, it suggests a weak constitution. If the line gets stronger after this marking, it suggests that good health has been restored.

A chain seen on the heart line may have physical implications, such as a weakened vascular system. Emotionally, it suggests that the subject has trouble forming and sustaining relationships.

THE CIRCLE

Students sometimes have trouble identifying a circle, for it can be confused with the island formation. Circles stand away from the palmar surface and do not touch a line.

As a rule, a circle is beneficial wherever it is found. On the Apollo mount it signifies success through natural talents, while on the Jupiter mount it implies success through learning. On the mount of Saturn a circle indicates good investigative powers; on the mount of Mercury it shows business flair.

However, a circle on the Luna mount, near a travel line, has a negative implication, suggesting danger through water. On the three occasions I have seen a perfect circle in this location, the owner was drowned.

If found near the heart line, under the Apollo finger, the owner may have visual problems. If under the mount of Saturn, there may be hearing or balance problems. A circle on the inner side of the life line, fortunately fairly rare, may imply serious vision problems. Traditionally, a well-formed half circle suggests trouble for one eye only.

MINOR MARKS

A variety of minor marks may appear on their own or in clusters on the lines or on the main palmar surface. They also appear on the sides and back of the hand. In Eastern palmistry these marks have endless connotations and interpretations. Western hand analysts tend not to view these marks with the same significance.

BELOW Chains on a line indicate a weakening effect – this chain on the heart line may imply vascular problems or an inability to commit during relationships.

life line

bar

ABOVE A bar cutting through the life line may indicate an emotional upheaval or trauma.

chains

heart line

ABOVE A circle on the Saturn mount indicates good investigative powers. The subject may be involved, for example, in medical research.

circle on Jupiter mount

RIGHT Circles are usually good signs – here the circle on the Jupiter mount shows benefit from studying.

THE CROSS

A cross is composed of two opposing lines of energy: literally, a crossroads which tells us to stop, look, and evaluate. Without exception, the cross is considered unlucky, signifying either loss or an accident. A cross touching any line has a debilitating effect, and if a line ends in a cross, the implied change of circumstances will be quite drastic.

A clearly defined cross, or series of small crosses, on the side of the nail phalange of the medius finger suggests a love of animals, and possible danger from them. A distinct St. Andrew's cross between the head and heart lines that does not touch either or both lines and has no influence marks touching it, is the *Croix Mystique*. This shows a love of the supernatural, especially when the mark appears directly under the middle finger. If it is under the first finger, the owner will use psychic powers to fulfill ambition. If the mark is found under the Apollo finger, the subject may become famous (or infamous) for abilities in a field related to the occult.

ABOVE The *Croix Mystique*, found between the head and heart lines, denotes those with a love of the supernatural or occult.

THE DOT

A dot can only appear on a line and, unless it is very large, it acts as temporary interference.

When everything seems to be going well but then, for some unknown reason, everything comes to an annoying and frustrating halt, there is probably a dot on the line relating to that aspect of the subject's life. If the line is clear after this temporary block, all will go well again.

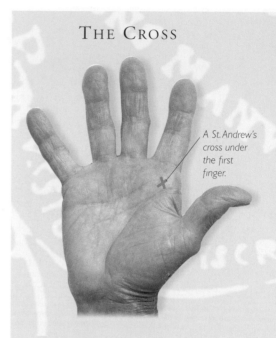

THE CROSS

A St. Andrew's cross under the first finger.

ABOVE A St. Andrew's cross under the Jupiter finger will enable the subject to use psychic powers to fulfill their ambitions.

THE GRILLE

The grille is a collection of crisscrossing lines almost always found on the mount of Venus. It implies a dissipation of power and energy. On Venus it suggests dissipation of the physical resources in futile pursuits.

On a full hand, a line that ends in a grille pattern weakens the resolve, while in an empty hand it suggests someone who can never manage to finish what he or she starts. This person needs supervision.

A grille pattern found on the mount of Jupiter indicates an owner with a cold nature. A grille on the first finger basal phalange suggests an owner who can become fanatical. With a grille on the Saturn mount, expect to find a lack of any real direction.

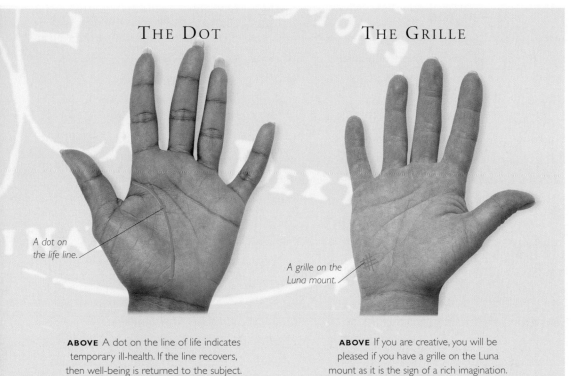

THE DOT

A dot on the life line.

ABOVE A dot on the line of life indicates temporary ill-health. If the line recovers, then well-being is returned to the subject.

THE GRILLE

A grille on the Luna mount.

ABOVE If you are creative, you will be pleased if you have a grille on the Luna mount as it is the sign of a rich imagination.

A grille on the basal phalange of the second finger implies an owner who will waste time on non-events or abandon projects altogether. On the Apollo mount, a grille denotes a vain subject with a misplaced belief in his or her own abilities.

When a grille appears on the basal phalange of the third finger, art may be distorted in some way. You might find this marking on producers or users of pornography, for example. A grille on the mount of Mercury indicates someone who will try to deceive but usually unsuccessfully, because he or she is so transparent.

A grille on the lower phalange of the fourth finger is not very positive, either. Its owner is prone to verbal excess – and is not always completely truthful. On the Luna mount, a grille enhances the imagination.

If the Mercury line passes through a grille, the subject will be given to tantrums. A head line ending in a grille implies diminished lucidity toward the end of life.

A grille on the second phalange of the thumb is very rare, but if it is found here, the subject may not always take everything into account when making decisions, especially important ones. There may also be a degree of self-deception.

Think of a grille as a collection of crosses where all the lines permanently oppose one another. Every good trait is undone by bad aspects. Little can come of anything, no matter how hard one tries.

ABOVE If a Mercury line passes through a grille the subject will be prone to tantrums and sulking.

THE ISLAND

Islands can only appear on lines and are an unfortunate mark. By their very appearance they must weaken the strength and resolve of the line on which they are found.

An island on the line of life weakens the constitution. There will be poor health for as long as it is present. If it frays or dissolves into tassels, health will decline accordingly. A life line that starts with an island, or a collection of small islands, indicates a sickly childhood or a youngster with little enthusiasm or energy. If the line begins in an open island there is mystery surrounding the subject's birth. Once the line strengthens, health and general zest for life also improve.

ABOVE A life line that begins with an island would suggest that the subject suffered regularly from illnesses during their childhood.

An island on the heart line suggests vascular troubles or hearing and visual problems. When the heart line starts with an island, especially an open-ended one, there may be a hereditary health problem or family weakness.

An island on the head line indicates poorly functioning mental powers for as long as the island is present. A head line that ends in an island indicates poor mental abilities at the end of the life.

An island on either the fate or the Sun line indicates lack of direction and weak resolve in career matters, or possibly a setback in the subject's career. Should either line end in an island, the subject's career may well end in misfortune and losses.

It is not helpful to have a Mercury or health line on the hand, and a health line with an island in it is even less desirable, for the island indicates an aggravation of the negative health condition. An island at the end of a health line may indicate the end of life. If you see such a mark, it is vitally important to use the utmost sensitivity when interpreting it to your subject.

THE SQUARE

A square can be a specific formation, or it may be made accidentally by lines crossing each other. Either way, it is usually favorable and is always a sign of preservation. If it occurs over a break in a line, whatever the difficulty, the subject will come through it safely. Always examine the line after such a difficulty occurs. If it remains strong there may be after effects, but there should be a recovery. The square will have done its part to help preserve as much as possible.

A square found on any mount helps protect the subject from any excess implied in the mount. A square on the mount of Jupiter is known as the teacher's square, for it confers an instinctive ability to lead and instruct. A square on the Saturn mount maintains balance. On the Apollo mount it suggests a traditional outlook in the arts. A square on the Mercury mount confers the gift of effortless communication.

In Eastern palmistry, a perfectly formed square just inside, but not touching, the life line on the mount of Venus represents a part of life spent shut away from others. An examination of the rest of the hand may show the nature of the confinement.

*An island on
the head line.*

THE STAR

A star indicates an intensification of a combination of energies. Generally it is a good influence, but if it is found at the end of a line it may portend real problems. Wherever a star occurs, its effect will never be forgotten by the owner.

On the life line a star indicates physical shock or injury; on the head line it shows a severe mental shock; and on the heart line it warns of a severe emotional matter or even a heart attack. Should all three major lines send branches to a central point and meet in or with a star formation nearby, the result of the suggested incident will seriously change the subject's lifestyle. The incident will never be forgotten, and if other people are involved, they will never be forgiven.

A star on the end of the fate or Sun line shows a career that will end either in brilliance or total disaster. Owners of this mark walk a tightrope all of their own making, and they know it. The huge gulf of difference between fame and infamy is the challenge that they must face, and they are often willing to take the gamble.

The presence of a star on any of the mounts intensifies the reading given by that mount. Any small influence lines leading to the star will give the hand reader clues to the origins of the event.

RIGHT An island on the head line suggests a period of mental disorder.

RIGHT A square over a break in the life line indicates a period of difficulty from which the subject will recover safely.

*A square over
a break in
the life line.*

RIGHT Those who have a star at the end of their fate line will either have a magnificent career or fail miserably!

*A star at
the end of
the fate line.*

ABOVE A square on the mount of Jupiter is the mark of an instinctive instructor. The palm of a general is likely to bear this mark.

THE TASSEL

The tassel is usually only seen at the end of the life and health lines. It indicates a weakening of the line's energy and generally appears in conjunction with the problems of old age. When seen at the end of any other line it shows a dissipation of the powers of that line. I have never seen a line re-form once a tassel sets in.

THE TRIANGLE

The difficulty with the triangle is that hand readers may mistake it for a poorly formed square. Although the triangle, like the square, is generally favorable, the two markings are otherwise extremely different. The presence of a triangle can indicate creative or intellectual talent connected with the area in which it is found. When found near a line but not actually touching it, the triangle enhances the line's power.

A triangle on the mount of Jupiter confers tact and diplomacy; on Saturn it indicates research or a behind-the-scenes job, possibly involving a high level of secrecy. A triangle on the mount of Apollo suggests a physically artistic or constructive career – such as a sculptor, perhaps, a masseur or even a body-builder. If the mark is low down on the mount, the owner will be known for work done with his or her hands.

A triangle on the mount of Mercury shows a political animal, someone who can wheel and deal in any situation. Astute and very perceptive, these people have natural leadership ability in business, too.

Elsewhere, the triangle shows a natural talent for getting the best out of people and oneself. There is always a gift for leadership. A triangle located anywhere in the zone of Mars shows a dauntless fighting spirit. Setbacks are never permanent, for these people soon bounce back to defend what they think is rightfully theirs.

THE TRIDENT

This mark has always been considered important in Eastern hand reading, but Western hand analysts have only taken an interest in it since the mid 20th century. We tend to notice the trident, or three-pronged fork, but usually only when a line ends in it. This formation is rare, but if present, it confers success and good fortune not only in relation to the line it is on, but also to the whole surrounding area.

SINGLE VERTICAL LINES

All single vertical lines, wherever they are seen, mark a special effort by the subject. Horizontal lines may be seen as negative, because they act like a long bar; vertical lines are a positive influence because they act like an arrow of ambition and represent the ways in which the subject has tried to better himself or herself.

THE TASSEL, TRIANGLE, TRIDENT, AND VERTICAL LINE

BELOW Those with a triangle on the mount of Jupiter are usually excellent diplomats.

A triangle on the Jupiter mount.

A trident on the heart line.

ABOVE A triangle on the mount of Apollo would suggest someone with physically creative skills such as a sculptor.

ABOVE A trident is very rare – such a mark on your heart line suggests a happy love life.

BELOW Vertical lines are a positive sign, indicating that the subject has endeavored to improve themselves in some way.

Vertical lines on the head line.

A tassel at the end of the life line.

ABOVE A tassel at the end of the life line shows the natural debilitation of the body's functions as we age.

ABOVE Business-minded people are likely to have a triangle on the mount of Mercury. This type may also have a flair for politics.

TIME IN THE HANDS

* * * * * * * * * * * * * * * *

FOR CENTURIES, THE most common complaint of hand analysts has been their almost total inability to establish an accurate dating system. However, there are several timing systems that have some merit.

But first a warning: all hands are not the same size. You must make allowances for individual variations of shape and size, and the paths individual lines take. A long life line on a long palm may reach to the edge of the skin pattern at the base of the hand. A short life line on a short palm may only reach halfway down the hand.

Traditionally, the length of the life line corresponds with 70 years, irrespective of the hand on which it is found, but this is obviously wrong. However, another part of the same formula suggests that the fate line crosses the head line at about 35 or 36 years and, curiously, this works in most cases.

BELOW A system of timing events in the hand, invented by the Gypsies, uses a compass and draws three arcs through the line of life.

age 10

Compass point

age 30

age 50

TIME ON THE LINE OF LIFE

There is another very old timing method, supposedly employed by the Gypsies. It is worth experimenting with, as in many hands, though not all, it can be remarkably accurate.

Having made a handprint, take a compass and place one point at the precise middle of the base of the first finger. Put the other end at the exact middle of the bottom of the middle finger. Keeping the divider point on the first finger steady, swing the other point down through the life line. The point will intersect the life line at about age 10. Still keeping the pointer steady on the first finger, extend the other end to the base of the third finger. Swing the pointer again –

where it crosses the life line is about age 30. Do the same for the little finger; the pointer will cross the life line roughly at age 50. Always use a print for this exercise.

Because life expectancy in past centuries was far less than it is today, the old chiromants did not take the system beyond age 50. This is just one of the difficulties the modern palmist faces in trying to apply old formulas. Research is being carried out, but until something more accurate is discovered the old systems are all we have. To confuse matters further, some hand analysts find these time scales may be equally accurate if they begin their timing estimations where traditionalists end theirs. The reader is invited to experiment. In other words,

THE LIFE LINE TEST

Draw an imaginary line from the middle of the base of the first finger straight down to the line of life – this should intersect at about age ten. So, from the beginning of the life line to this point represents the first ten years of life. A brief question-and-answer session will establish accuracy and allow you to continue in a similar vein.

A second imaginary line drawn from between the base of the first and second fingers to the life line will cut in at about age 20. Similarly, a third line drawn from the base of the middle finger to the life line should cross at about age 35 or 36.

Beyond this, the system fails if the life line does not sweep this far out into the individual's palm. Nevertheless, if the previous calculations have been accurate, it is a relatively easy matter to gauge time on the rest of the line.

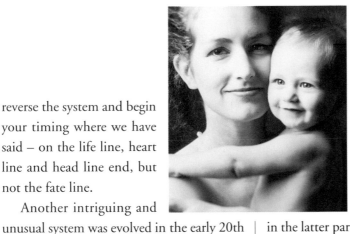

reverse the system and begin your timing where we have said – on the life line, heart line and head line end, but not the fate line.

Another intriguing and unusual system was evolved in the early 20th century. Place a length of thread on the life line and follow it all the way. Cut the thread at the end of the line. Then fold the length of thread in half and place it at the start of the life line. Where the folded thread now ends represents the age of 36 years. Mark this point lightly on the print that you have already made or on the hand itself. Dividing the top half of the line in two gives an approximate 18–20 age point. Dividing this

segment in half indicates roughly nine to ten years.

By carrying out a similar exercise on the lower half of the line, you will be able to time events in the latter part of the life. This method can also be used on both the fate and Sun lines.

This divide and subdivide method is often very accurate, but unfortunately it does not work with everyone. However, you now have a couple of ideas that may help you approximate the timing of events in subjects' lives with a fair degree of accuracy. Try the basic question-and-answer system to get started. You may find that it helps things quickly fall into place.

LEFT The dating systems can help prepare for some of the major events in our lives such as the advent of motherhood.

BELOW Traditional palmistry estimates times in the hands on the basis that life expectancy was much shorter.

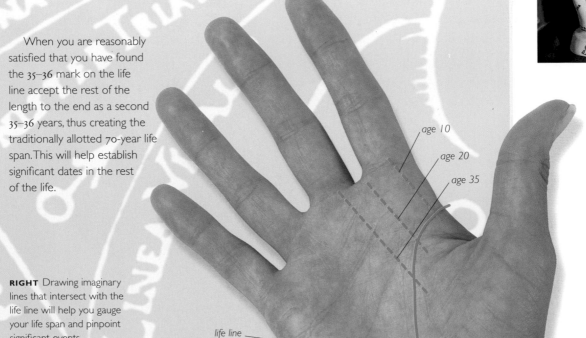

When you are reasonably satisfied that you have found the 35–36 mark on the life line accept the rest of the length to the end as a second 35–36 years, thus creating the traditionally allotted 70-year life span. This will help establish significant dates in the rest of the life.

age 10

age 20

age 35

RIGHT Drawing imaginary lines that intersect with the life line will help you gauge your life span and pinpoint significant events.

life line

TIME ON THE FATE LINE

No matter how long the fate line is, where it actually crosses the head line, or would cross if it were long enough, is about age 35 or 36. Where it passes over the heart line is roughly age 45, and the space between the heart line and the bottom of the medius represents about 25 years.

The length of the line, real or imaginary, between the head line and the base of the hand should be divided into two; this gives an approximate location for age 18–20. Divide this space in half again on either side for ages 9–10 and 36–40.

The same measurement method can be applied to the Sun line. This fairly basic system will, with practice, help you time events on either of these lines with reasonable accuracy. Again, it does not hurt to pose a simple question here and there during an interview.

RIGHT A Gypsy palmist scrutinizes the hand of her subject. Using the timing system on the fate line, the reader can predict what fate has in store, now and in the future.

ABOVE This sun dial represents an alternative method for measuring time. Timing on the Sun line is the same as that on the fate line.

RIGHT Time can be measured in the line of fate according to where it crosses the head and heart lines.

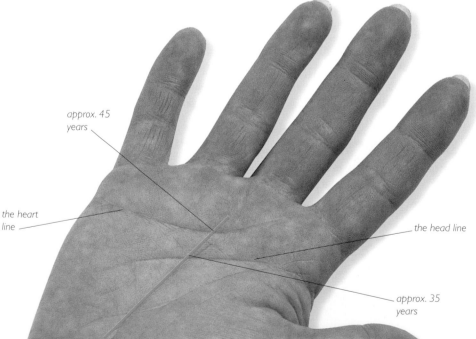

approx. 45 years

the heart line

the head line

approx. 35 years

TIME ON THE HEART LINE

Traditionalists claim that the heart line begins on the Jupiter mount, but as we have shown elsewhere, it may start anywhere on the radial side of the hand, and it may begin in a fork or even a three-pronged trident shape. Because there is no logical place to start measuring, it is nearly impossible for calculations on this line to be accurate.

There are those who say that you cannot time events on the heart line at all, because of what it represents. Others insist that to time events properly one should start at the outer edge of the hand and work inward toward the radial side. Each faction in this debate has its own merit.

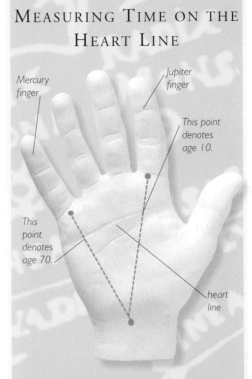

MEASURING TIME ON THE HEART LINE

Mercury finger

Jupiter finger

This point denotes age 10.

This point denotes age 70.

heart line

LEFT The Gypsy method for reading time on the heart line involves drawing an imaginary line from the Mercury and Jupiter fingers toward the bottom of the palm.

The Gypsies did have a traditional way of measuring time on the heart line, but – as modern hand analysts agree – it was severely limited.

First, you must draw an imaginary line from the center of the bottom of the Jupiter finger to the central point of the bottom of the palm. Do the same from the central base of the Mercury finger. The point where the line from the Jupiter finger crosses the heart line is said to be ten years of age – provided the heart line is physically there and does not start too far into the hand. Where the line from the little finger crosses the heart line represents 70 years. The midpoint between these intersections represents age 35–36.

Whether this method allows for finer approximations of time can only be determined by experimentation on individual hands. Try it and see.

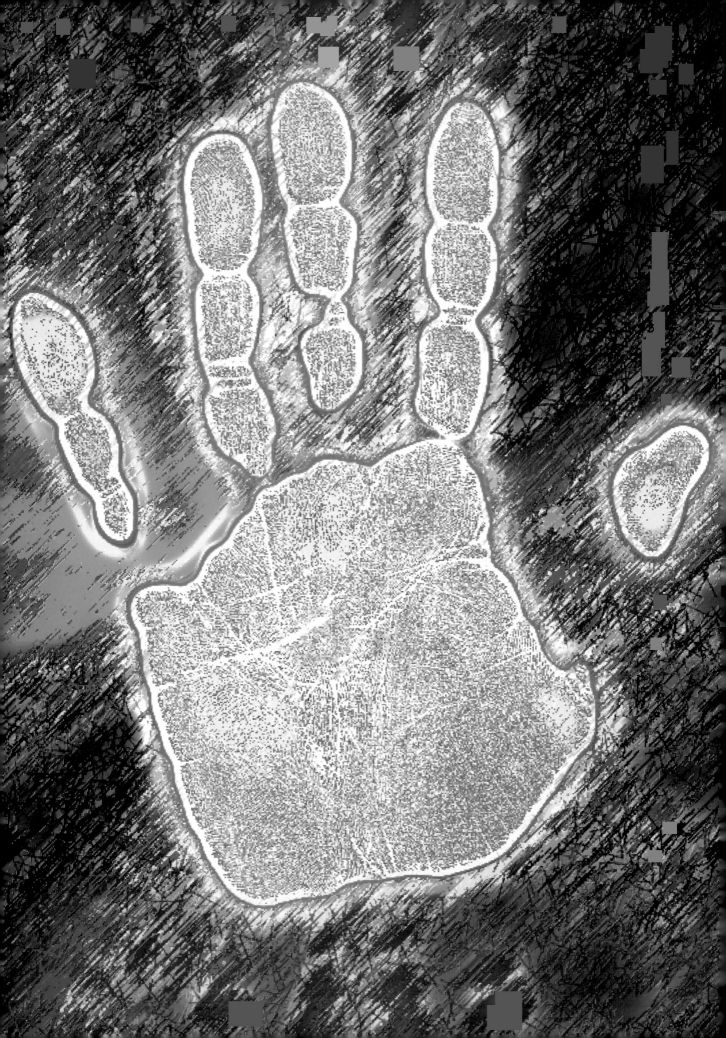

PART FOUR

PATTERNS IN THE SKIN

★ ★ ★ ★ ★

An individual's fingerprint and hand patterns take shape in the first few months of a person's life; after that they never change. They are often still observable even when all other features have deteriorated, and may be the only way of identifying someone after death.

While these markings are unique to each individual, they are made up of a series of definite patterns, which have been classified for purposes of personal identification, medical research, and hand analysis.

The very first textual references to these patterns were concerned with determining the central point of the digital mounts. Another feature referred to by early authorities was skin texture.

ABOVE Everyone has unique hand and fingerprints, and it is possible to identify distinct patterns that reveal traits in our character.

There are two distinct types: rough or open, and smooth or closed. The rough or open texture appears in the hands of people who prefer activity and concrete matters. When the pattern appears closed and fine to the touch, expect to find someone more refined and genteel in whatever activity he or she pursues. Skilled in the gentle arts of persuasion, someone like this will often be able to run rings around others.

THE FINGERPRINT PATTERNS

* * * * * * * * * * * * * * * * *

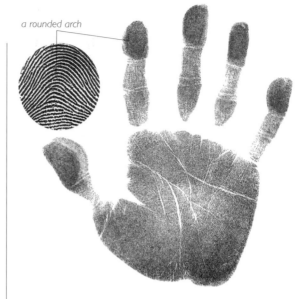

a rounded arch

THERE ARE THREE basic types of fingerprint: the arch, the loop, and the whorl. Each of these can be subdivided into smaller variations, and each has a different bearing on personality and character. A set or majority of a particular type of pattern will reveal the predominant personality trait.

RIGHT The arch is more commonly found on the subject with square hands.

THE ARCH

The arch can be shallow or very rounded. People with arch patterns are capable, trustworthy, and reliable characters who can cope well, especially when things go wrong. Occasionally they can seem stuffy or suspicious, but basically they are the salt of the earth. They will not be browbeaten into doing anything, for they stand their ground well and can be extremely stubborn. They do not make friends readily, but once they give their trust they are loyal and devoted. If this trust is betrayed in any way, the relationship will never be the same again, because although these people may eventually forgive, they certainly do not forget.

When the arch is found on the index finger the person is very much a realist, down-to-earth and intense. Although such people may be slow starters, they can shoulder responsibility and power as though born to it.

On the middle finger, the arch reveals a do-it-yourself type with the gift of being able to improve anything in his or her surroundings. These people, however, are emotionally repressed or inhibited. They

ABOVE It is best to use a magnifying glass in order to look at a fingerprint in true detail.

cannot or will not discuss personal problems, so personal relationships can be one-sided, especially if things go wrong.

A third finger with the arch pattern suggests constructive and practical types who can turn their hands to most things. Down-to-earth, they are usually unable to appreciate abstract matters. With support elsewhere in the hand they make excellent gardeners or may be involved in other outdoor pursuits.

It is rare to see an arch pattern on the fourth finger; if it does appear here, it may be one of a set. This formation confers practical business or communication skills. Though slow to start, once they're up and running, these people just keep on going. When the fingertip is pointed or supple, the subject seems never to stop talking and is unable to keep secrets.

The arch pattern on the thumb signifies self-preservation at all costs. Again, down-to-earth, sensible, practical, and with plenty of common sense, these folks can be found working in areas where these attributes are

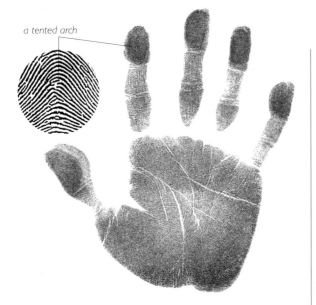

a tented arch

both ends. Impulsive, these people quickly become caught up in the mood of the moment. They live for the present, rather than stepping back to see where they might be heading. Even if they did know what was ahead of them, they probably wouldn't change their course of action.

On the middle finger this pattern reveals a predisposition to follow causes. Easily led, these people are utterly convinced they are doing the right thing and are not at all concerned with the rights and wrongs of their impulsive actions. In fact, they are not always even aware of mundane matters or normal responsibilities.

A tented arch on the third finger implies a volatile and emotional nature, often someone involved with the arts. He or she may even be gifted, perhaps not as an artist or performer but more likely in some sort of supporting role. These people may also be known for their appearance; their unusual dress and idiosyncratic mannerisms.

On the little finger the tented arch implies a subject who can easily interpret what others say or do. He or she knows what people around them want and is usually able to give it to them. In business, little escapes these people, and they seem to have a natural flair for making money.

On the thumb this pattern indicates adaptability and flexibility. Social animals, they have many friends and acquaintances. They prefer jobs that allow them to work in a variety of locations – anything that means novelty and change appeals to them.

LEFT The tented arch is a variation on the arch and belongs to the subject who is enthusiastic.

best employed – in the armed services or in public utilities such as the mail service. It does not pay to argue with this type unless you have all the facts.

THE TENTED ARCH

This variation on the arch pattern looks as if a tall, slim loop has been pushed up inside the basic arch and raised as far as it can go.

Overall, this type is much more enthusiastic than those who show the ordinary arch pattern. "Reform" could be their middle name. They want to change things, to set everything to rights as quickly as possible. These are the idealists who incite and inspire others but take little action themselves – they lead from the back. Full of charm and flattery, especially when they want something, they are not always known for their tact and diplomacy at other times. Anything highly innovative or unusual attracts them.

When the tented arch is found on the first finger, the owner can lead a dangerously full life, frequently burning the candle at

BELOW A policeman, such as a British "Bobby", is likely to have arches on several fingers. Arches denote a trustworthy, steadfast character.

THE LOOP

There are two basic types of digital loops, the ulna and the radial. If you think of the loop as a lariat, the ulna loop starts or is "thrown" from the percussion, or little-finger side of the hand, makes the pattern, and returns to the start. The radial loop starts from the radial, or thumb side of the hand, makes its pattern, and returns to its starting place.

Overall, either loop indicates a flexible and adaptable type of person who is ready to compromise and makes a good team worker. Although there are some fairly basic and straightforward differences between the loops, a loop of either type on a specific finger will display the personality traits specific to that finger, tempered by the characteristics peculiar to the type of loop.

People with ulna loops are usually not self-starters. As a rule, they are more followers than leaders and need to be prodded into action by someone more assertive. They act instinctively and may give way under pressure.

Those with radial loops, however, have more initiative and are far more self-interested. They always have their own ambitions in mind when they undertake a new project. Under pressure, these folks dig their heels in and resist.

A loop on the first finger suggests an improviser who inspires by example. Good leaders, flexible, open to suggestion, and very thoughtful, these people always consider the needs of others when making their plans.

Someone with a loop on the middle finger may be drawn to anything unusual, such as the occult or mystical matters. Such people tend to be withdrawn and do not make friends too easily. They are inclined to be changeable and bend with the wind.

A loop on the third finger denotes an owner who responds to all things beautiful, someone whose profession may in fact be in the beauty industry. Impatient souls, they dislike waiting and can throw nasty tantrums if they do not get everything now. The lower on the tip the loop is located, the more they may flout convention or set out to shock, largely in order to make themselves the center of attention.

A fourth-finger loop indicates a highly impulsive nature. Much is promised but little is actually delivered, largely because these people are prone to taking on more than they are able to handle. When they realize what they have done they are instantly contrite, but by then it is too late. A high-set loop on this finger will attract the

BELOW Loops on the thumb show good diplomatic skills in the subject.

DIGITAL LOOP PATTERNS

ABOVE Radial digital loop (left hand). People with a predominance of this pattern are self-starters and show potential leadership skills.

ABOVE Ulna digital loop (right hand). The ulna loop is thrown in from the percussion (little finger) side of the hand and denotes a follower.

ABOVE In some loops the ridges about the core converge to give it a whorl-like appearance.

ABOVE This rare pattern, in which the ridges bend over like a wilting flower, is known as the Nutant loop.

BELOW Good team workers, such as sportsmen and sportswomen, are bound to have the loop pattern on several of their fingertips.

subject to the world of communications, while a low-set loop, especially with a round tip, suggests humor.

Loops on the thumb show diplomatic skills. Those with a radial loop will have a positive nature, while those with an ulna loop will be more impulsive. A weak-looking thumb with either loop can be easily led; a strong thumb belongs to the opposite type.

People with short fingers, a long palm, and a full set of loops start much and finish little. They can also lack self-control.

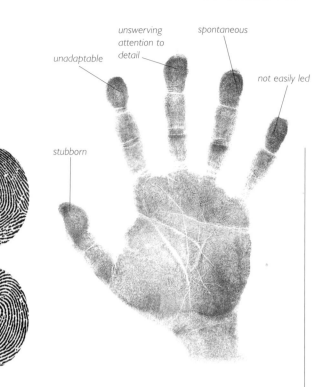

unadaptable

unswerving
attention to
detail

spontaneous

not easily led

stubborn

ABOVE Whorls
on certain fingers
denote particular
character traits.
Inflexible types
who are often
highly individual are
likely to have the
whorl pattern on
most fingers.

THE WHORL

The whorl pattern suggests a fixed and unyielding nature. These are highly individualistic, often inflexible people who feel they must do things for themselves. A high-set pattern emphasizes this outlook, while a low-set whorl relaxes it somewhat.

Wherever found, the pattern suggests a cold or unapproachable type who seems to find it difficult to be open. It is rare for these people to delegate work, as they feel they will do the best job and cannot trust anyone else to do a better one. Their one saving grace is that they are good in emergencies.

People with a whorl on the first finger are not very adaptable; they can never be told what to do – they have to be asked. They have an ambitious nature, which often eclipses everything else. The higher set the whorl, the more the owner is inclined to specialized work. A low-set whorl indicates a good teacher in a specialized subject.

A whorl on the middle finger indicates an owner who is rarely diverted from his or her chosen path. Inflexible by nature, he or she revels in research or investigative work

that requires attention to detail. If such people have long fingers and a short palm, they may have such an eye for detail that they can drive others to distraction and be unbearable to live with.

On the third finger the whorl suggests strong individualism and an unconventional outlook. These people make good designers in an artistic field of some kind. They can, however, lack spontaneity in social situations and are difficult to get to know intimately. They are very demanding taskmasters who always ask for, and somehow obtain, loyalty from all those with whom they work.

A whorl on the little finger shows that the owner will not be easily influenced. He or she prefers firsthand experience to secondhand gossip. These people operate best behind the scenes, where they create a powerful web of activity; little escapes them.

A whorled thumb implies a stubborn character, someone not easily sidetracked. Opposition means nothing – once these people start something, nothing is allowed to get in their way. Quite materialistic but with excellent taste, they live and work in pleasant surroundings.

THE VARIATIONS

The basic whorl pattern is largely a series of concentric circles, often with a flat base, and usually with two tri-radii points at the base. There may be a composite whorl, with a loop and/or arch within the outer circle. A twin or double-looped whorl is exactly that – two small loops that flow in opposite directions within the outer circle. Other variations are for the most part known as

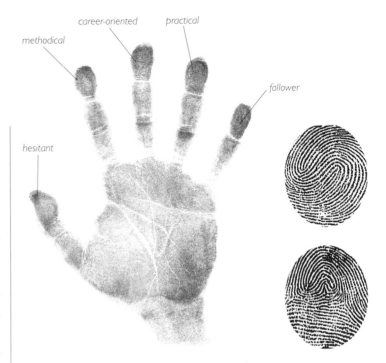

methodical

career-oriented

practical

follower

hesitant

compound whorls, which have many similar implications to the "normal" whorl pattern, but with some slight differences.

Composite whorls indicate someone with better-than-average practical skills. These people are able to see both sides of a question, often even before the question has been articulated. They are always open to opposing views and suggestions and prefer not to accept anything at face value – firsthand experience is what counts.

A composite whorl on the first finger suggests an inner emotional conflict and a lack of social adaptability. These people may take time to come to a decision, but when they do they stick with it, rightly or wrongly. They plan well and can be very methodical, especially if they have a long index finger.

On the middle finger, the composite whorl is a strong indication that career matters. These folks don't like to get involved with people they meet through their work. They have a very clinical approach and may be a little too matter-of-fact for most people.

A composite whorl on the third finger denotes basic tastes and a dislike of unnecessary ornamentation. Practical artistic pursuits are favored, along with plain food and straightforward people.

A composite pattern on the little finger detracts from fluent expression, especially in emotional states. These people let others lead.

On the thumb a composite whorl indicates hesitancy and uncertainty. These people can work hard and play hard, but planning their way through any project is not their forte. As a rule they have low tolerance levels and are not very flexible.

Twin-looped whorls are quite rare, especially on the thumb, but wherever they are found they represent a "push-me–pull-you" type of approach within the scope of the finger on which they appear. They switch moods dramatically and will have problems when it comes to reconciling opposing viewpoints.

Variations in whorl patterns may be read as ordinary whorls, for they are so rare it has yet to be established if they have any individual interpretations.

In summary, it is best to look for the dominant pattern – that found on at least six fingers – as the principal expression of the overall personality. However, it is not clear-cut – look to the hand shapes for further clues. Four loops are more at home on a conic hand. Similarly, the arch is far better suited to a square hand shape, while whorls go well with knotted fingers, and so on.

ABOVE A composite whorl generally indicates someone whose practical skills stand them in good stead.

ABOVE A composite whorl on the Apollo finger denotes those who are practical artists and have simple tastes and leanings.

121

THE APICES

* * * * * * * * * * * * * * * * * *

WITHIN THE CAPILLARY lines and furrows of the palmar surface, the skin ridges form patterns. Hand analysts have studied these closely and have found that each pattern represents certain personality traits.

Each of the digital mounts – Jupiter, Saturn, Apollo, and Mercury – has a central point, or apex, that can be traced relatively easily, and that can be used to analyze individual behavior. The apex of the mount of Venus is usually obscured by a grille pattern and is therefore not so easy to find.

To locate the central point of a mount, examine the skin pattern until you can trace what appears to be a a roughly triangular formation. The apex is at the top of the triangle. It does not have to be directly under the finger and in fact rarely is.

Occasionally mounts may merge and appear to be one elongated mound sharing two fingers. When this happens, there will

be an inclination toward one finger or the other, and a central point must be established. When the apex is nearer the index finger than the medius, read it as a Jupiter/Saturn mount with that emphasis. Should the apex be nearer the middle finger, read it as a Saturn/Jupiter mount. The same sort of emphasis should be given to other pairings. An apex may be high, low, or centrally placed.

THE MOUNT OF JUPITER

A centrally placed apex here suggests personal pride, integrity, and a strong sense of responsibility. However, if the apex is more toward the thumb side, there will be an adventurous streak combined with a dislike of petty bureaucracy. An apex displaced toward the middle finger reflects far more respect for authority, and responsibility is second nature to the subject.

If the apex is low set, the owner may lean toward a career in the armed forces or a service industry such as the mail service. A high-set apex suggests that the "correct" way of doing things is of utmost importance to the subject. Mental or intellectual matters tend to attract the subject as a hobby or recreational pursuit.

THE MOUNT OF SATURN

As a rule, the apex of this mount is high set and often leans toward the Jupiter or Apollo fingers. A centrally placed apex on this mount indicates someone whose feet are firmly on the ground and who has a strong sense of right and wrong. Likely to be self-reliant, this is someone who stops and thinks

RIGHT If the skin pattern on the mount of Jupiter leans toward the thumb expect to find an adventurer.

things through before rushing off into action. He or she does not trust too readily and will look a gift horse in the mouth!

An apex that leans toward the first finger implies an ambitious nature and, perhaps, an interest in some sort of collecting. This person is quite serious. Should the apex lean toward the third finger, the nature is less serious and more sociable.

With a low-set apex, expect to find an interest in practical outdoor pursuits like gardening. If the apex is high set, the owner is almost always practical and good with his or her hands.

ABOVE A high-set apex on the Jupiter mount suggests someone who is a stickler for correctness.

Saturn mount

Jupiter mount

Venus mount

Apollo mount

Mercury mount

Luna mount

LEFT To find the apex of a particular mount look at the skin pattern and find a triangular formation at the central point of which is the apex.

ABOVE The gregarious type is likely to have an apex on the Mercury mount that leans toward the thumb side of the palm.

THE MOUNT OF APOLLO

If this apex is in the center of the mount, there is a good practical artistic nature; these people are inclined toward crafts such as sculpting, painting, or potting. If the apex is low set, the subject's career may still involve these interests, but he or she may have trouble mixing socially. If it's high set, there will be a love of nature and perhaps a gift for dealing with animals.

Should the apex lean toward the middle finger, the owner does not trust others readily and can be reticent in some situations. Such people are fairly deep, and may be emotionally inhibited; it may take a long time to get to know them intimately.

An apex that leans toward the middle finger is the mark of a natural salesman, one who has a talent for making – and losing – money. The further the apex inclines to the ulna side of the hand, the more the owner is likely to bend the rules to suit his or her own interests. In some cases this can indicate a typical con artist.

THE MOUNT OF MERCURY

It is rare for this apex to be directly under the mount. Usually it leans toward the Apollo finger, and these two fingers may even share the mount. If, however, the apex is centrally placed under the little finger, the owner has a gift for communication. Reading, writing, linguistics, and languages are all attractive to this person. If the apex leans outward, toward the percussion, the attraction becomes a passionate love. With an apex that leans toward the inner hand, this love is less intense and gives way

THE APEX ON THE LUNA MOUNT

Often, though not always, the base of the palm contains a tri-radius that marks the line between the mount of Venus and the Luna mount. This configuration tends to favor the Luna mount. The apex may be near the top of the arch of the horizontal ridges in the skin pattern along the base of the palm.

If the pattern is present, the lower and more centrally placed it is, the less its effect seems to be. But the higher in the palm it appears, the more likely there may be cardiovascular problems.

When placed quite low, no more than an inch (two to three centimeters) immediately above the bracelets, the subject will have a practical, matter-of-fact approach to life. Should the tri-radius be higher, no more than two inches (five centimeters) up from the base of the palm, expect to find the kind of possessiveness a collector might display. If the apex is even higher, just under the head line in the middle of the palm, the nature is less materialistic and calculating, perhaps more liberal-minded and idealistic.

If the line of life merges or blends with the apex, there may be some restriction in the subject's life, or his or her career may be connected with the family. If it is just outside the life line, however, the subject should be fairly free of familial restrictions.

RIGHT A high tri-radius pattern on the Luna mount suggests the possessiveness of a collector.

A very high apex suggests idealism.

A higher apex denotes possessiveness.

Luna mount

Venus mount

ABOVE Check the position of the apex on the Luna mount. It may be intersected by the main palmar lines.

A low apex denotes a practical character.

If the fate line passes through the complete configuration, the owner's career may be plagued by problems for as long as the patterns are merged. If the Sun line blends with the pattern, the subject is likely to experience disappointments with regard to his or her hopes and wishes.

If this tri-radius merges with or just touches the Mercury line, health problems may be aggravated. The lower along the line they merge, then the more likely the health defect is to be physical rather than emotional.

to social relationships; the owner will be outgoing and popular in a crowd.

A low-set apex suggests a basic ability to communicate. High-set apices indicate an interest in abstract subjects. Whether high or low set, the personality of the subject may seem slightly quirky or unusual in some way.

THE MOUNT OF VENUS

If there is a tri-radius on this mount it is often difficult to locate, because there is usually a grille formation in the central part of the mount hiding it. However, if you do find one, note the position. If it's centrally placed there will be a healthy libido and a generally friendly nature. If it's low, the subject will be inclined to follow his or her more basic drives. A high apex can indicate a prudish owner. Look for clues in the rest of the hand for confirmation of any of these particular traits.

THE NEPTUNE MOUNT

On the mount of Neptune the apex seems to have little effect, but should the life line end, or the fate line begin, within the mount, the subject will always have a special affinity with nature and the outdoors. It has been suggested that an apex on the Neptune mount is the mark of an astrologer, a palmist, or one involved in a similar spiritual occupation. It is also seen on the hands of those who practice acupuncture, shiatsu, and other alternative therapies.

BELOW If the life line begins or the fate line ends near the apex on the mount of Neptune, its owner will have a love of nature, like the botanist Carl Linnaeus portrayed here.

THE SPECIAL PATTERNS

* * * * * * * * * * * * * * * * *

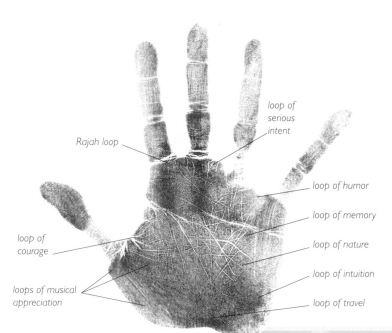

loop of serious intent

Rajah loop

loop of humor

loop of memory

loop of nature

loop of intuition

loop of travel

loop of courage

loops of musical appreciation

RIGHT There are a number of loops on the surface of the palm that may reveal specific character traits and major life events.

BELOW The name "Rajah loop" originated in India where palmistry has a long history.

THERE ARE OTHER patterns found at specific points all over the palm's surface. Interpretation of these other marks will depend on the exact nature of each pattern, together with any special formations it may contain. Do check carefully and consider all the options before you state your findings. For example, if musical appreciation is suggested, it does not necessarily have to be classical music, nor should musical ability or proficiency be assumed. It may simply mean that the subject derives great personal pleasure from music in some form or another.

There are three main inter-digital loops that enter the skin pattern at the top of the palm. These are the Rajah loop, which enters between the first and second fingers; the loop of serious intent, between the second and third fingers; and the loop of humor, which comes in between the third and fourth fingers.

THE RAJAH LOOP

The name comes from Indian palmistry and is said to signify royal blood, probably because it is usually found on the hands of natural leaders.

For example, rebel leaders who seize power after a long and weary battle, and who then stay in power, often have this mark. Those who try and fail, or who do not last long, tend not to have it.

The Rajah loop may appear on one or both hands and always refers to qualities of leadership. If it appears on the right hand only, the subject works hard for social position and achievement. If it appears on the left hand only, then these benefits come naturally.

If the loop appears on both hands, the owner will enjoy respect and social standing as a matter of course. Such people do not yield to adversity; they are stoics and fight back bravely if things don't go according to plan. They are likely to have an engaging, almost magnetic personality, so that others follow them naturally. But be warned, they do not suffer fools gladly.

THE LOOP OF SERIOUS INTENT

This mark indicates a particular goal connected with a serious hobby or other interest that dominates the subject's life. The person will wait patiently, for many years if necessary, knowing that one day that goal will finally be achieved.

When the loop is on the left hand only, the goal is usually not actively pursued, and the subject is content to wait for his or her chance to shine. If the loop is on the right hand only, the owner will work diligently toward the desired aim. When it occurs on both hands, the subject will display a driving ambition and will pursue his or her goal no matter what, refusing to be thwarted by any obstacles that might block their path.

Whatever the interest, it often begins as a hobby that, as time goes on, consumes the owner more and more. Other people may become involved, especially if it is a kind of service, and a grateful recipient may offer a small payment as a gesture of goodwill. From here, it is only a matter of time before the pastime develops into a small business, and from there it escalates into the full-scale obsession for which the subject is known.

THE LOOP OF HUMOR

This can be a small loop or a fairly large one – sometimes it may be a large, rambling swirl mainly under the third finger. Wherever it appears, it confers a cheerful disposition and a sense of humor. The larger the loop the more likely there is to be a sense of the ridiculous as well.

Occasionally the loop has a slightly square appearance. In these cases the owner will be noted for his or her graceful and gentle nature. These people never knowingly offend or upset, and are known for their politeness and good manners. Natural mediators, they can stop disputes of almost any kind by sheer force of personality. Because of this, their reputation will grow and their services will be sought, whatever field they may be in. This loop is often seen on the hands of good personnel officers, troubleshooters, and counselors.

If the loop is found in both hands, all these traits are enhanced. On the left hand only it shows a natural gift for mediation and counseling. On the right hand only this mark suggests even more pronounced gifts, and a heightened sense of humor.

Should there be a swirling collar formation under the third finger on either or both hands, the person may be very touchy, unable to abide criticism no matter how well meant. However, he or she will feel quite free to criticize others at the slightest provocation.

THE LOOP OF COURAGE

Often, this is a barely discernible loop in the skin pattern that enters the palm between the thumb and first finger on the mount of Mars. It represents courage in some form. A short loop suggests an appreciation of adventure limited to an occasional foray into the local countryside or outdoor exercise with others – hiking, hill climbing, or orienteering, perhaps. The further into the palm the loop goes, the more physical or

ABOVE The loop of serious intent marks the dedicated pursuit of a goal – usually related to the subject's hobby.

moral fortitude the subject displays. He or she may be engaged in some sort of continuous uphill battle against almost insurmountable odds. Should the loop touch the family ring, the central issue will be a matter of family honor. If it should touch the line of life, it may be a struggle caused by poor health.

THE LOOPS OF MUSICAL APPRECIATION

Under the thumb, at the side of the Venus mount, a loop may be found under the angle of time on the lower phalange of the thumb. This shows an appreciation of music and rhythm, although not necessarily realized. Another loop, not always clearly seen, may be noticed toward the middle of the mount. This may suggest a preference for stringed instruments and orchestral music.

If there is also a loop that enters from the angle of harmony, the subject will usually have good general musical knowledge and a natural ear. This loop may be present with or without the other two.

THE LOOP OF INTUITION

A loop that enters the base of the hand and throws its lariat onto the mount of Neptune indicates natural intuition and an uncanny way with people or animals.

If the loop touches the fate line, the subject will have fatalistic tendencies and will be fairly resigned to his or her lot, putting duty and obligation first. If the line of life enters the loop pattern, the owner is probably in a caring career of some kind and makes a loyal friend.

ABOVE The loop of musical appreciation doesn't necessarily denote those who perform: the subject may simply derive a great deal of pleasure from music.

RIGHT The loop of intuition, found on the mount of Neptune, might belong to an animal lover.

THE LOOP OF MEMORY

This is found in the center of the palm on the Luna mount, and will touch or run with the head line. Whether found on both hands or just one, it denotes a good memory.

On the left hand only it shows an ability to remember past events quite clearly. If it's on the right hand only, the owner is selective about when he or she uses the gift. If the head line ends in the middle of the loop, there will be almost total recall – but only if the owner chooses to draw from the past.

If this loop is slightly higher in the hand, between the head and heart lines but not touching either, there will still be a good memory. If the loop sweeps further down into the Luna mount the subject will possess some sort of specialized knowledge enhanced by their ability to recall facts.

THE LOOP OF NATURE

A loop that enters much higher on the Luna mount from the percussion edge confers a great love of nature. It may be expressed in gardening, outdoor activities with animals or nature, or even something as unusual as dowsing ability. A loop on both hands accentuates the gift.

THE LOOP OF TRAVEL

If there is a loop that enters the skin pattern from the outer edge of the hand, quite low down the Luna mount, travel of some sort will be an important part of the subject's life. If the loop is on both hands, the importance of travel will be accentuated.

THE ARCH OF
EMOTIONAL EXPRESSION

A clearly defined arching in the skin pattern immediately above the heart line and below the little finger indicates a person who has difficulty expressing emotion in public. This person doesn't like to hold hands with his or her partner while out, and isn't comfortable kissing or hugging anyone hello or good-bye. In private these people are perfectly normal and may even be emotionally intense. In public, they freeze.

THE ACTOR'S WHORL

There may be a whorl in the skin pattern on the Luna mount that doesn't interfere with any other mark or line. It just lies there in the open field of the mount. This is the mark of the actor, who completely submerges his or her personality in that of a character.

The person may not be a performer in the obvious sense, but simply someone who can take on a role for some purpose – a courtroom lawyer, for example, or a good teacher and orator. If the hand is weak, the person may possibly use the ability for criminal purposes such as fraud.

THE ARCH OF SOCIABILITY

In the same place as the actor's loop you may instead find a tented arch in the skin pattern. This shows great sociability, someone who is an asset at any gathering.

However, if there is just an ordinary arch here, the opposite will apply. This marks the owner as one who makes and keeps to his or her own set of rules. If you cannot conform to those rules, this person will not be fazed.

THE FIELD OF INDIVIDUALITY

If there are no markings at all on the Luna mount, just a plain open field in the skin pattern, the subject is free of complexes. These people do not worry about anything, are open and straightforward, and expect others to be the same. It is occasionally suggested that these people have limited understanding, but this is inaccurate. These people are down-to-earth and practical, so decision-making is quite basic. Subtlety may be lost on them, but little else is.

All these special marks and patterns sometimes appear in some form or another. They do not all show at the same time. It is their formation blended with the state/condition of the hand upon which they do appear that helps in analysis and conclusions.

On a good hand, therefore, the pattern will indicate the better side of the subject's nature. When found on a poor hand it usually refers to negative tendencies.

ABOVE The actor's whorl, found on the Luna mount, does not necessarily confer the gifts of a performer; it may mark the palm of a lawyer or compelling orator.

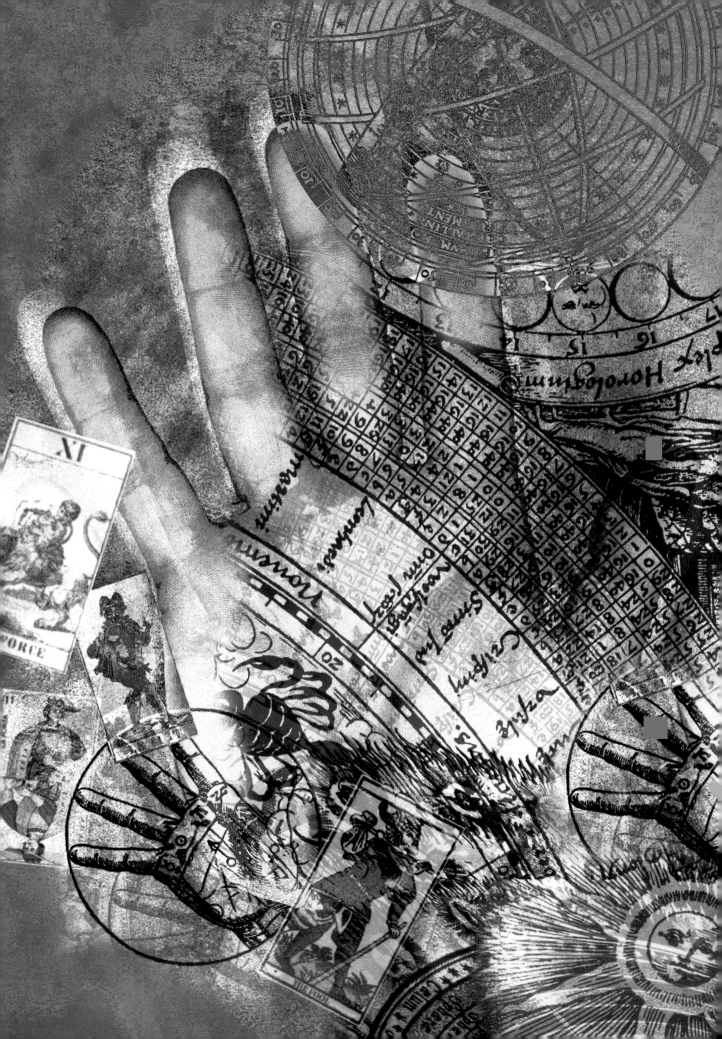

PART FIVE

PRACTICAL PALMISTRY

★ ★ ★ ★ ★

The way is now open for you to experiment with all your newfound knowledge. Practice on yourself first. Through palmistry you can learn about your strengths and weaknesses and discover where your talents really lie. You can also monitor your health so that you can be sure of having enough stamina to face testing times that lie ahead.

With good powers of observation that are regularly practiced, you can learn to assess other people. All sorts of clues to what lies ahead can be detected in a person's hands. The palm even contains potential answers to those questions that arise as we grow and mature.

ABOVE Having become familiar with all the different aspects of palmistry, it is now time to apply your knowledge.

The palm can be studied to give further insight into certain isolated aspects of life, be it personal relationships, career, or matters concerning money. And should you wish to take your studies further, hand analysis can be practiced in conjunction with other disciplines involving character analysis: clear links with astrology, graphology, numerology, and Tarot have been researched and published.

RELATIONSHIPS

★ ★ ★ ★ ★ ★ ★ ★ ★ ★ ★ ★ ★ ★ ★ ★

OUR FIRST RELATIONSHIPS are those within the family circle. It is here, more than anywhere else, that a child learns how to get along with other people. Observing how his or her parents and other family members relate to one another, and reacting to other people in the immediate environment, are a child's first experiences of relationships, and these experiences are carried forward into adult life.

A child's position in the family hierarchy plays an important part, too. As a rule, eldest children have more confidence, whether they have been pampered, spoiled, or strictly disciplined.

Second children are often less confident, but likely to have been more aggressive in their efforts to prove themselves by outdoing their older sibling. Given time and careful guidance, these children usually have no trouble finding their niche in life.

Third and subsequent children usually learn how to cope with the hard knocks of life quite early. There is sibling rivalry in any family, and the more brothers and sisters there are, the more rivalry there is likely to be. So third and later children have to work hard to succeed.

Even at a very early age, a child's hand will show signs of confidence or a lack of it. Whether the child is a natural leader or a follower can be detected very quickly. Children's hands reflect their changing attitudes as they learn to control, fight, or compromise with life and the constant challenges that they face as they grow up.

ABOVE A child's position in the family and his or her relations with siblings as well as parents plays an important role in his or her formative years.

RIGHT It is possible to tell at an early age if a child is going to be a follower or a leader. If the fingers are well spaced they will show initiative.

HANDS OF A LEADER

To assess a child's leadership potential, look first to the thumb on both hands. A well-developed thumb, properly positioned, with a good angle to the index finger, shows good personal control, which in turn helps in controlling and leading others. A strong right thumb partnered by a weak left thumb is a sure sign of strong character and good personal control.

When relaxed, the thumb and forefinger should form an angle of between 45 and 90 degrees. The wider the angle, the more self-reliant and sensible the child is likely to be. There will be good self-discipline and a natural sense of responsibility. This configuration in a child's hand indicates a positive nature, an innate sense of justice, and the ability to see both sides of most arguments. The level of judgment will, of course, vary with age. If the angle between the thumb and forefinger exceeds 90 degrees, the child will be inclined toward foolhardy actions – he or she may take chances where others would not.

Look at your child's thumb for a clue to strength of character.

The lower the thumb is set on the side of the hand, the stronger the inspirational side of the nature will be. If this low-set thumb also has a wide angle it indicates a child who is always ready to explore and who has a strong sense of self-preservation. A low-set thumb with a narrow angle nearly always indicates someone actually skilled at self-preservation. This youngster will use every trick in the book to survive.

A high-set thumb shows creativity. This child learns early in life to solve problems in original ways. Often, there will be a flair for the unusual. Children with a high-set thumb and a narrow angle will also do whatever they can to protect themselves, but they will do it with their own original style.

A wide space denotes independence.

HANDS OF A FOLLOWER

Obviously we cannot all be leaders. There have to be followers and, as with leaders, there are different types.

If the Mercury finger is very low set, the child may be convinced that he or she is inadequate or inferior in some way. Such children may shun social life and pick friends very carefully because of difficulty in expressing their emotional needs.

A low-set index finger also suggests a lack of self-confidence in the subject's general approach to life. These children want recognition, but seem unable to get it because they step back from self-promoting activities, and hesitate to put their own ideas forward. If both fingers are set low on the hand, the child needs a lot of affection: he or she is easily hurt by words or deeds.

Narrow spaces between the fingers are also significant. A narrow space between the index and medius shows that the child prefers to remain one of the herd. He or she complies with the majority and either cannot or will not step out of line.

A narrow space between the middle and third fingers indicates an underlying sense of caution. The youngster has personal security and the future firmly in mind at all times; it would be rare for him or her to be rash or act impulsively.

A narrow space between the third and fourth fingers indicates a sense of dependency. A young child whose hand shows this configuration will always need constant reassurance in everything he or she does. Such children tend to copy others around them whom they think are superior in some way. They are often very sensitive to mood or atmosphere.

LEFT Dependency or, conversely, the need to be individual, shows in the spacing of children's third and fourth fingers. The little finger will be angled away from the hand if your child is very independent.

BELOW Even your youngest child's hand will reveal their budding character traits.

HEALTH

* * * * * * * * * * * * * * * * *

THE BASIC SHAPE of the hand reveals a lot about health and can show a predisposition to certain weaknesses, which may manifest either physically or psychologically.

Children with a Fire hand, for example, can be impulsive and have a tendency to not look where they are going, so they are likely to be somewhat accident-prone. They may not always be capable of sustained effort, because they burn up their reserves of energy much too quickly.

Children with the Earth hand worry too much. Problems with diet, digestion, and, later in life, the bowels are not uncommon. It is therefore especially important for parents to make sure these children always have an adequate and balanced diet. They also need plenty of exercise and fresh air.

Youngsters with Air hands need to learn to pace themselves and not take on more than they can deal with at any one time. Their overactive minds don't seem to be aware that their bodies can burn up energy quickly. When they start using their energy reserves, the weakest part of their constitution begins to suffer.

Children with Water hands are delicate, emotional, easily led, and prone to all sorts of illnesses, real and imaginary. Stomach disorders and allergies are especially likely. These are the sort of children who will read about a certain disease and then convince themselves they have all the symptoms the next time they don't feel well.

Whatever hand shape a child has, it pays to check the fingertips regularly for "white lines," a sign of temporary illness or stress. Children with weak physical constitutions often show these markings. Also, if you think a youngster doesn't seem quite right, look at his or her nails. If the nails are pale and longitudinally ridged, there may be a nervous problem. If the nails are also bitten, the child is probably a born worrier who cannot let go of problems. Ferocious nibbling demands urgent attention. Remember, what may seem trivial to an adult may be quite serious to a child.

A child whose palm shows bars that cut either the heart or head line very likely suffers from anxiety and built-up inner tensions. If head and heart lines begin

RIGHT A child whose palm shows bars crossing the head or heart lines is probably suffering from nervous tension.

bars crossing heart line

bars crossing head line

A "mouse" or bulge indicates good health.

and continue together for a short distance, this is accentuated. The child has little self-reliance, is a worrier, and is probably on the defensive nearly all the time.

A hand that is "full," that is, covered in a fine tracery of tangled lines going in all directions, is another sure sign of a worrier. This child lives on a knife edge: he or she is hypersensitive, and the wrong word or action can be enormously upsetting. The head line may have a fluffy appearance, suggesting an inability to cope with stress.

Signs of physical ill health, especially in a child, may initially be detected by checking the "mouse," the little mount found bulging at the back of the hand between the thumb and the first finger.

When the thumb is held close to the hand or clenched into a fist, a small bulge is created between the thumb and first finger at the back of the hand. If this little mount is firm to the touch, it shows good health. When the mounts on both hands are full and firm, the child has zest and enthusiasm for life. If they are flat or soft, the child may be under par. Tiredness caused by a long, busy day or working at a task that required close attention to detail or a lot of physical effort can cause this mount to soften. It will regain its firm consistency after a good night's rest.

However, if the mount always seems soft to the touch, the child may have a weaker than average constitution. Such a child is likely to catch frequent colds, and if there's a "bug" going around, he or she will get it. Recuperative powers are usually weak in this type of child.

Test the zone of Mars as well. This is the area in the center of the palm that lies below the digital mounts and between Luna and Venus mounts; it includes the mounts of upper Mars and lower Mars, and the plain of Mars. When this area is well developed, the child has very good powers of resistance and large reserves of energy – in fact, the amount of energy that these children can expend is astonishing to other lesser mortals!

The life line on a child's hand is also revealing. A weak, islanded, or chained line suggests a weak constitution, or poor health for as long as these features are present. Should the line become stronger and sweep out into the palm, the child's recuperative powers will strengthen and health will improve in later years.

ABOVE Ask your child to form a fist keeping the thumb resting on the back of the first finger. A "mouse" or bulge should appear between thumb and finger which, if firm, denotes good health.

LEFT Feel the hands for firmness or boniness. When the mounts on both hands are full and fleshy your child is full of the joys of spring!

HUMOR

* * * * * * * * * * * * * * * *

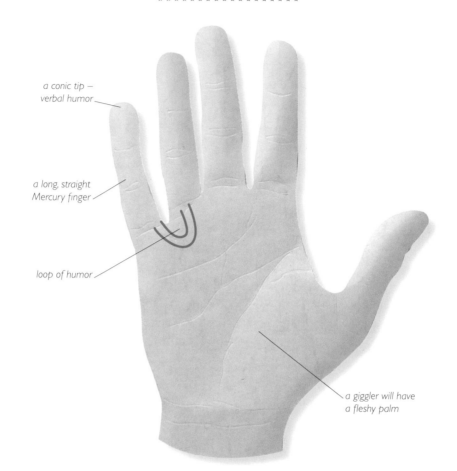

a conic tip – verbal humor

a long, straight Mercury finger

loop of humor

a giggler will have a fleshy palm

ABOVE Those with soft palms are likely to be unstoppable gigglers.

The subject of humor has been avoided by most palmistry writers, so the guidelines offered here are based on my personal experience and research.

The dictionary defines the quality of humor as "a comic, absurd, or incongruous quality causing amusement," or "the faculty of expressing or appreciating what is humorous or comical." It is not difficult to detect humor in the hand; what is not so easy to determine is the level of humor in an individual's makeup.

The longer the little finger, the more readily the subject will express humor verbally. A rounded tip adds to this; those with a square tip tend toward dry humor. Subjects with spatulate tips express humor more actively, as in practical jokes. They may not always instigate pranks, but (pardon the pun) they often have a hand in them.

The softer the hand, the likelier the owner is to be a giggler. The firmer the hand, the better the ability to keep from dissolving into giggles at awkward moments.

A supple and flexible little finger indicates a well-rounded sense of humor. These types appreciate literary humor and puns; limericks and poems composed by them are usually well received.

A square tip on the Mercury finger modifies humor. It has its place, but it must be kept in check. Such people have a poor

sense of fun and almost no natural sense of humor. They do not let go easily or make fools of themselves. They also tend to make poor practical joke targets.

Those who have a spatulate tip on the fourth finger always appreciate the funny side to life. Laugh with these people – but remember not to laugh at them.

The best way to assess purely mental wit is to look at the length of the little finger in relation to the rest of the hand. The longer the finger, the more cerebral the wit; the shorter the finger, the more down-to-earth the sense of humor.

There may be a little loop in the skin pattern between the third and fourth fingers. This is the loop of humor (see page 127), a sign that the owner has a strong sense of the ridiculous. A loop on both hands shows an appreciation of farce.

Occasionally, this loop will partially cross over the Apollo mount, indicating one of two traits. Either the owner has a natural sense of the ridiculous and happily finds fun in most things, or the humor is quiet and subdued. People in the latter category cannot understand others who do not have the same approach. Their mood can turn sour very quickly if they are not supported, and they get touchy if criticized.

Sometimes the loop in the skin pattern swirls all the way over the Apollo mount, as if cutting the finger off from the rest of the hand. These people enjoy humor and express it easily. If this pattern is found on the left hand only, the subject enjoys life, and not much gets him or her down. When it's on the right hand only, the disposition is largely the same, but with a more ready wit.

Supple, flexible hands imply an easygoing nature. These people take things as they come. There is usually not much self-discipline, and an inborn lazy streak restricts their sense of humor.

Firm, stiff, or unyielding hands imply quiet humor. If the Saturn or Mercury mount is well developed, the subject's sense of humor may be difficult for others to appreciate. This sort of humor will have a philosophical leaning, which can be an acquired taste for some people.

A "full" hand, with a fine tracery of lines running all over the palmar surface, indicates an imaginative approach. These people see humor everywhere and in everything. The mind is rarely still, and it is difficult for them to switch off.

LEFT The practical joker or clown is likely to have a spatulate tip on their little finger.

RIGHT A sense of the ridiculous, perhaps understood by Laurel and Hardy, is expressed in a largish loop found in the skin pattern between the third and fourth finger.

SEXUAL DEVELOPMENT

* * * * * * * * * * * * * * * * *

HANDS ARE MORE likely to show basic sexuality than most people realize, for hand reading is not just about shape, line formation, and other such features. So much depends on how we use our hands to express ourselves in close encounters of the sexual kind as well.

From infancy we learn to use our hands to express our emotions. Our feelings of anger, caring, horror, love, sorrow, and surprise are molded very early in our lives through our contact with other people and the world around us. We use our hands to explore by touch, not just everyday objects, but also ourselves. When we start to learn about ourselves sexually – so often at the wrong moments, according to many parents – it is a natural progression to learn more about others as well. We learn to use our hands when we make love, for the human hand is unique in being an essential part of physically expressing our deepest emotions and feelings. A look at our hands reveals basic drives, urges, and our capacity for giving and receiving love and affection.

The shape of our hands reveals our overall sexual personality. People with square hands are conventional in their sexual needs and desires. Dependable and straightforward, they are liable to get caught up in routines and habits – even in their sexual expression – that are hard to change. Much more practical than romantic, they keep both feet squarely on the ground, and they make good providers.

ABOVE If your lover has square hands, don't expect any surprises! They prefer conventional relationships.

ABOVE A conic hand belongs to someone who is impulsive and sensitive. They are quick to fall in and out of love!

Don't expect those little personal touches or gestures of closeness to be demonstrated in public, for this type always seems aware that others may be watching. This is no reflection on their strength of feeling – those with the square hand are simply more private than most.

People with round or conic hands are innately romantic. They are very impulsive,

People with spatulate hands are unpredictable and not noted for their faithfulness. They start relationships with great zeal, but if the object of their affections is not equally ardent, they just look elsewhere for the next flirtation.

Those with pointed hands are often out of touch with the real world when they fall in love. They put their lover on a pedestal, and nothing can convince them that he or she may have flaws. Born romantics, impressionable, captivated, and led by their own extremely vivid imaginations, they make wonderful lovers if they manage to find the right partner. The firmer the hand, the more control they exercise. The softer the hand, the more inclined they are to hedonism, although this is found more among those with the spatulate hand shape.

ABOVE Those with spatulate hands fall "truly, madly, deeply," but if this is not reciprocated they give up quickly.

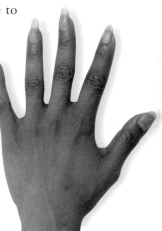

ABOVE True romantics have pointed hands, but are often victims of their over-active imaginations.

LEFT A great deal of love and affection is expressed through the hands.

extremely sensitive to atmosphere, color, shape, and sound, and may be prone to falling in and out of love often – almost daily in extreme cases! They are so changeable in their affections that many with this hand shape are capable of keeping more than one romance going at a time – quite openly and honestly in many cases. That is not to say that they are not loyal.

A well-developed Venus mount indicates a healthy libido with an instinctive and easy display of affection. If the mount is overdeveloped in relation to the other mounts, the subject will be uninhibited, perhaps even oversexed, and not mindful of his or her manners when in company.

A flat, lifeless look to the mount of Venus indicates poor emotional responses. These people are not good social mixers; they are so difficult to get along with that they fare better on their own. Basically selfish, they are not good at sharing.

If the Luna mount is high and fleshy, there is a richly developed emotional side to the imagination. It is hard to tie these people down to one partner at a time. They are so restless that they find it hard to sustain interest in a relationship.

An overdeveloped Luna mount suggests a changeable nature. Willpower is often poor – the subject is easily sidetracked. With a flat or low Luna mount, the subject is emotionally cold. He or she is not likely to have much imagination and can be utterly insensitive to the wants and needs of others.

People with flexible hands are easily influenced, impressionable, and easily controlled by others. They may have some difficulty remaining faithful during a relationship. Hands that are only moderately flexible show emotional versatility. Such people are a little more in command of themselves and reliable in relationships. They are very adaptable.

Those with stiff, unyielding hands are inflexible and selfish, and have great difficulty expressing themselves emotionally, mentally, and physically, even when they are alone with a partner.

Broad, healthy-looking hands show a good commonsense approach to all sexual matters. A closed, pale, and narrow hand shows just the opposite.

When the head line and the life line are joined at the beginning, there is always some uncertainty in emotional expression when it comes to emotional matters. People with this configuration (and sometimes their partners as well, for they tend to choose similar types) are very sensitive to external influences. The wider the space between these two lines, the less they are concerned with their partner's needs. They may have a selfish streak, along with a tendency to antagonize people close to them without realizing it. Tact and diplomacy are often lacking.

The longer the head line, the more mental control overrules emotional needs. If the line turns slightly upward at the end, the nature can be very cold indeed.

When the heart line is low on the hand, with a good clean sweep outward toward the percussion, the emotional and sexual life is open, warm, and very affectionate. The higher the line sits on the hand, the colder the subject's nature.

Many fine lines dropping away from the heart line suggest a person prone to falling in love with love, but never quite able to enjoy a satisfactory and lasting partnership.

BELOW If the Luna mount is fleshy and noticeably high, there is a highly developed emotional side to the subject. He or she is likely to be romantic but hard to pin down.

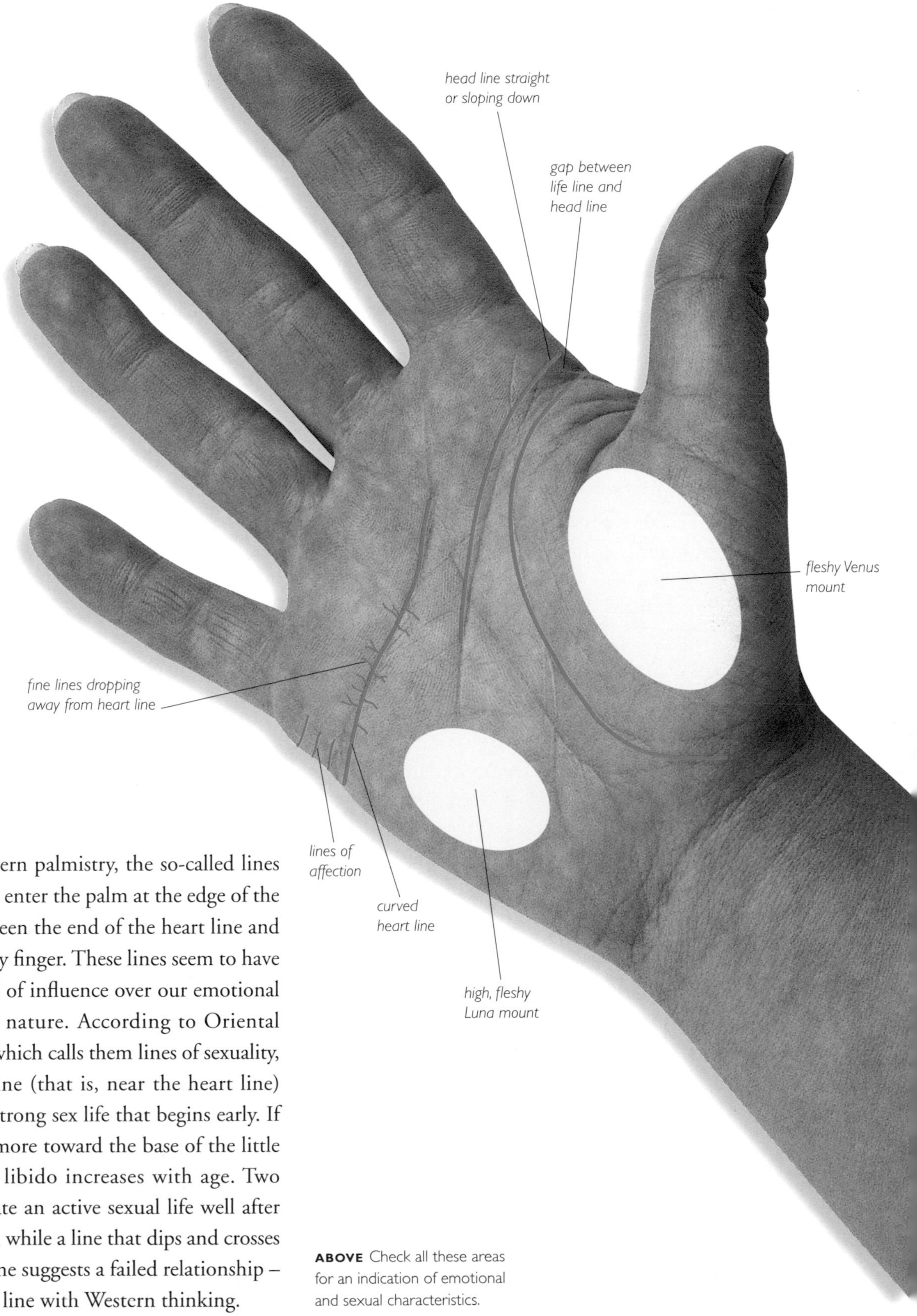

head line straight
or sloping down

gap between
life line and
head line

fleshy Venus
mount

fine lines dropping
away from heart line

lines of
affection

curved
heart line

high, fleshy
Luna mount

In Western palmistry, the so-called lines of affection enter the palm at the edge of the hand, between the end of the heart line and the Mercury finger. These lines seem to have a great deal of influence over our emotional and sexual nature. According to Oriental palmistry, which calls them lines of sexuality, a low-set line (that is, near the heart line) suggests a strong sex life that begins early. If the line is more toward the base of the little finger, the libido increases with age. Two lines indicate an active sexual life well after middle age, while a line that dips and crosses the heart line suggests a failed relationship – which is in line with Western thinking.

ABOVE Check all these areas for an indication of emotional and sexual characteristics.

141

CAREER

★ ★ ★ ★ ★ ★ ★ ★ ★ ★ ★ ★ ★ ★ ★ ★ ★ ★

AFTER PUBERTY, AND with school behind us, the next stage in our development is usually working for a living. For generations, most youngsters were expected to follow parental wishes by entering the family business or favored family career, regardless of their own feelings. However, those days are gone. Most children now expect and get active parental support in following their own aspirations.

By studying the hands of youngsters and following basic palmistry techniques, it is possible to determine whether a child needs a gentle push or stronger encouragement in a particular direction.

Most of us choose a career in one of several major fields: the arts, business, manual or practical work, the sciences, and the professions. Each of these has a series of subdivisions, which in turn may be further subdivided into different approaches. So if a child is drawn, for example, to a career in the arts, you may want to determine whether he or she would do better in a creative role or an interpretive one. When a youngster opts for a life in business, his or her talents may be better directed to accountancy than to sales.

RIGHT A square hand denotes a down-to-earth approach to career and ambition.

square hand

When someone's hands are assessed, the palmist cannot necessarily say what the subject currently does for a living. What a skilled analyst should be able to detect, however, is where the subject's natural flair and potential lie.

Those with square or rectangular hands are apt to be among the most realistic in their approach to their career, and to life in general. People with this configuration are consistent, dependable, and resourceful. Usually well balanced, with plenty of sound common sense, they are open and straightforward. They make excellent employees, for they see and tell things the way they really are.

ABOVE Hand analysis will reveal a vocation – be it in the arts or sciences.

BELOW Those with conic hands may have wonderful creative powers with potential to be channeled into an artistic career.

conic hand

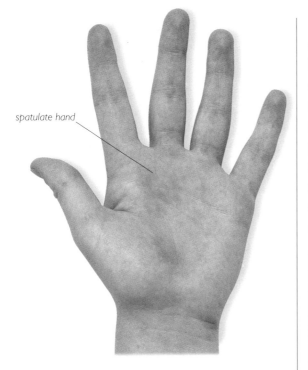

spatulate hand

Youngsters with philosophical or analytical hands are completely different. Practical and coldly logical, they are able to analyze absolutely everything. As long as they think a project makes sense they will go ahead with it with enthusiasm and a sense of purpose, but if it is flawed they'll step back, reject the thing altogether and look for something else to occupy their time. They are dependable and very efficient, with diplomatic skills to match.

LEFT Those with spatulate hands are likely to inspire admiration in others with their easy eloquence.

Those with conic hands are receptive to the mood of the moment and, while not always practical, can have tremendous creative powers. They have a talent for picking up the "vibes" around them, and they are able to adjust their expectations and actions accordingly.

The person with an active or spatulate hand is an opportunist. Children with such hands show leadership qualities at an early age. They also decide early on who might be a threat or a challenge to them. Astute, independent, but self-centered, they have one principal interest: how they can get ahead – and stay there. These folks have an inborn executive streak; they make natural politicians and good speakers. They know how to get people to follow them, for they inspire with easy rhetoric.

Those with pointed hands need to be very carefully schooled when discussing career directions. To start with they are largely unsuitable for the everyday cut and thrust of the modern world. These people would be better off in design or decorating fields for they do far better as "backroom" boys and girls. Some do extremely well in the acting world – they have the gift to totally immerse themselves in their roles.

ABOVE Children with philosophical hands are practical and logical; they are likely to grasp scientific subjects, such as computing, with ease.

MONEY

★ ★ ★ ★ ★ ★ ★ ★ ★ ★ ★ ★ ★ ★ ★ ★ ★

GENERALLY SPEAKING, CAREER success leads to money and position. Money is of major importance to many people, regardless of what their hands may imply. But there is a basic "attitude" toward money that can be detected in most hands. People with firm hands, for example, are willing to work hard to earn money, whereas those with soft hands are likely to have a lazy streak.

Some feel that luck and money are closely related, but this is not necessarily so. "Luck" is not born of thin air. If anything, hard work is needed to create luck, or at any rate to capitalize on it. Traditionally, a hollow or bony feel to the center of the palm is said to reflect bad luck. When a subject's palm is resilient and full, however, he or she will have his or her fair share of luck.

Owners of Fire hands seem constantly to have their share of luck and good fortune, but they are wise and spread their money and assets around for a variety of reasons. They simply do not like to put all their eggs in one basket. If something instinctively "feels" right they will put their support and their money behind the project.

People with Earth hands work and play hard and put their money away for a rainy day. However, many of these people are extremely reluctant to dip into their reserves, even if it is pouring. These people need to be reminded that you can't take it with you.

Those with Air hands are philosophical when it comes to money and financial matters. They are ready to take a calculated risk and are not averse to trying something new if they think it has a fair chance of success. They should not be considered gamblers in the strictest sense of the word; they just seem to have a natural flair for speculation.

People with Water hands will say they are not really interested in finance, gambling, or any other form of speculation. In most cases they are being honest – they are not materialistic. But of the four groups, these people are the most likely to have healthy bank balances.

Each individual finger can also tell us a great deal when it comes to material matters. Either collectively or on their own, they will reveal our attitude to the way we manage our assets.

The long Mercury finger shows business acumen and a talent for commercial affairs, while a long Apollo finger implies a gambling instinct.

RIGHT, ABOVE
People with Earth hands have lots of energy for work and will save up their cash fervently.

ABOVE Money is of importance to most people, whatever a reading of their palm might suggest.

RIGHT, BELOW
A long Mercury finger shows business acumen and a definite talent for commerce.

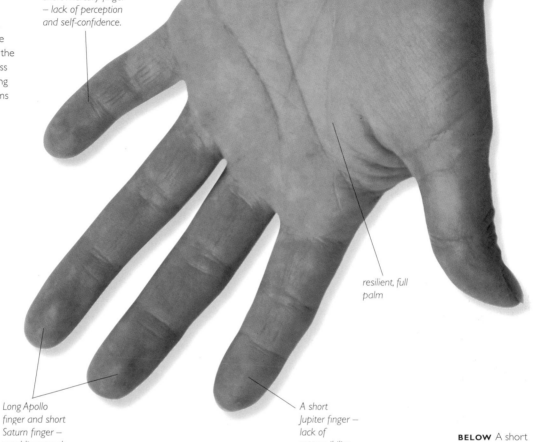

Short Mercury finger – lack of perception and self-confidence.

resilient, full palm

Long Apollo finger and short Saturn finger – gambling streak.

A short Jupiter finger – lack of responsibility.

The long Saturn finger reveals a cautious nature, and a long Jupiter finger shows good sense; if the Jupiter finger is also straight, personal integrity and honesty are implied.

The subject with a short first finger has a poor sense of responsibility; a short middle finger can reveal a secret gambling nature. A short third finger implies pessimism in money matters. Those with a short fourth finger will either lack perception or have little confidence in their own decisions – assuming they are able to reach the point where they make a decision in the first place.

TRAVEL

★ ★ ★ ★ ★ ★ ★ ★ ★ ★ ★ ★ ★ ★ ★ ★ ★

THERE ARE MANY restless spirits in this world, eager to travel, explore, seek new experiences, and meet new people. And there are those who, while they may be fascinated by the idea of travel, are less eager in their search for new horizons. They may venture forth, but they feel a need to be back in their homes by nightfall.

The bigger and wider the hand, and the larger the Luna mount, the less routine matters will attract the subject. There is an inherent need to keep on the move, a constant urge for travel. The owner is restless and dislikes any sort of restriction. In some cases, life may be lived on the run.

ABOVE Some people are fascinated by travel but will not relinquish the security of their homes to which they happily return.

ABOVE Unusual forms of travel – like air ballooning will appeal to those with a fleshy Luna mount on a large palm.

RIGHT The Luna mount is traditionally associated with travel and will bear certain signs.

A long life line that sweeps out onto the Luna mount.

lines across the Luna mount

Luna mount

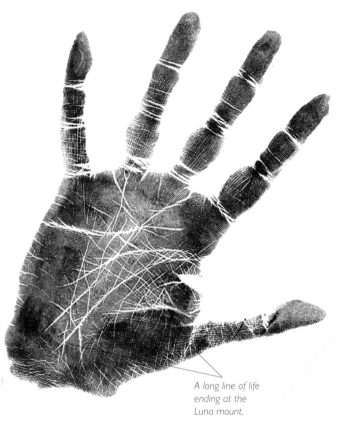

A long line of life ending at the Luna mount.

Another sure sign of travel, probably overseas, with a chance of staying there, is a bold, distinctly etched horizontal line across the Luna mount from the percussion. Smaller, shorter lines can also suggest overseas travel, but these would be shorter and less important journeys, such as those a courier might make. A large number of small, distinct horizontal lines on the mount also suggest that much of the life will be spent in travel – again, probably overseas.

Tradition says that a line of travel curving downward toward the wrist indicates travel-related risks. If the line turns upward, however, it means a rewarding end to the journey. A travel line that either touches or cuts through the line of life is traditionally said to indicate danger through water travel. Today, I would venture to include danger by sea and air as well!

A line of life that swings out into the palm and ends on the Luna mount is another sign of a strong love of travel. A fork at the end of the line is an additional sign of restlessness. If the line ends on the bottom of the Luna mount, the owner will be up and away at a very early age, and this type is likely to settle abroad.

ABOVE If the line of life ends at the base of the Luna mount, the subject will very probably emigrate.

RETIREMENT AND OLD AGE

* * * * * * * * * * * * * * * * *

AFTER YEARS OF activity in our working life, the time comes for most of us to retire and, hopefully, to settle down happily. This affects us all in different ways. Some take early retirement, while others actually dread the whole idea. For some, retirement is a golden age when they will have time to do all the things they have always promised themselves. Others fear that the lack of income might restrict their lifestyle. There may also be worries about losing contact with former workplace colleagues and having to make new friends.

People with square hands cannot settle properly after giving up work. They are so used to a regular routine that any change is upsetting to them. If they are used to being outdoors, it may help a little; for them, getting used to any new pattern of life in retirement causes problems.

Those with round or conic hands are so stimulated by new experiences that they soon forget how they used to live. As a rule they do not plan too far ahead and cope well with the transition.

People with spatulate hands hardly notice not going to work – they soon pack another 25 hours into the day with all their new activities. As long as there is something to occupy both mind and body, they slip easily into new ways of doing things.

Those with philosophic hands edge into retirement with a great deal of caution. Some of these people might prefer to stay busy by working part-time as a consultant.

Once retired, it does not hurt to keep an eye on the lines on the hands. As long as they are strong and seem supportive of the new lifestyle, retirement should hold few problems. When a line begins to show signs of deterioration, activities associated with the line should be eased back.

spatulate hand

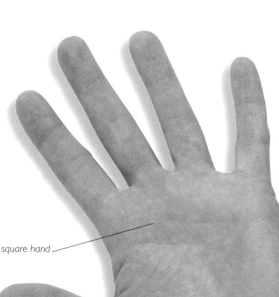

ABOVE Those with spatulate hands will soon be absorbed by activities and will fill their retirement days with ease.

RIGHT For those with square hands, retirement is an anomaly – they are so used to routine that such a massive change is rather traumatic for them.

FAR RIGHT Retirement may be a time for catching up on all the chores that had previously been neglected.

square hand

And there we have it. This brief look at how our hands reflect our reactions to the various ages and stages of life was designed to show you what to look for to make analysis easier. Of course, it hasn't been possible to cover all experiences and aspects of life, but the guidelines set out here will help you experiment with the subjects we have had to leave out. The more you practice, the easier it becomes.

philosophic hand

149

GESTURE AND BODY LANGUAGE

* * * * * * * * * * * * * * * * *

THE VAST MAJORITY of us show our real nature in the way we speak and use gesture. People's personal "sign language" – the way we use our hands and bodies in our communication with others – provides the basis for a study all of its own.

We begin learning this sign language unconsciously as babies, and we adopt it almost as a reflex action. It does not take long to see the impact a particular sign or movement has on those around us. What we do or say with our bodies may capture our parents' attention, make them laugh with delight, or provoke their anger. As we get older, we may start to use gesture and body language consciously for our own purposes.

When we speak with others we also listen and pick up little clues from each other's gestures. Without necessarily realizing it, we can give and receive myriad silent messages with facial expressions alone. The way we slightly shift our feet, move our hands, even the way in which we hold our heads reinforces these signals, either emphasizing or contradicting what we may be saying. An entire science of body language and gesture has developed to study and analyze this form of communication. As a science within a science, it has now also become an integral part of the palmist's study.

One aspect of gesture is handwriting, which has been described as an observable result of consistent gestures shaped by the intelligence and emotional state of the writer. Handwriting is one of the very few natural body movements that cannot be completely altered by conscious attempts to disguise it. A study of basic handwriting styles and character analysis techniques will be of great help to anyone aspiring to be a palmist (see pages 170–171).

INTERPRETING GESTURE

The interpretation of gesture is not universal. The same movement of a hand or finger can have totally different meanings in different countries. It can be quite an experience in a foreign country to make a familiar gesture to a traveling companion only to find you have insulted the locals, albeit in innocence.

Hand gestures may be categorized into four groups: emotional, intellectual, nervous, or social. As a rule, most gestures by either sex are of an emotional nature, either offensive or defensive.

The pointing forefinger with the clenched fist is a most emphatic and unmistakable gesture. Look at the person's other hand for signs that he or she is about to lose control. If the other hand is still open, then once the person has made the point, he or she will probably ease back. If the hand is closed, be prepared for possible physical aggression or even direct attack.

This gesture is interesting. The index finger always points and accuses elsewhere, but the rest of the fingers all curl up and point back at the accuser, as if acknowledging some of the responsibility. In many cases this is so. Remember this the next time someone points an accusing finger

There is a close relationship between Palmistry and Graphology – perhaps not surprising, since the two disciplines are so directly concerned with the hand. In a great many cases, the shapes and patterns of a person's hand are reflected in his or her handwriting.

ABOVE

Handwriting is the most instinctive form of gesture; even conspicuous alterations will not disguise its meanings.

at you – if you start to refute the argument at this point, you may well be able to defuse the tense situation.

Hands held close against the body may indicate some kind of introversion. Perhaps this person is insecure and uncertain, and is too often on the defensive. In contrast, flamboyant extroverts will swing their hands in wide expansive gestures, suggesting they know what they are doing. Hands in pockets are as suspect, as are those that are hardly ever used to support a point.

When a plea for innocence is made by someone holding his or her hands open but with the backs toward you, you can be certain that nine times out of ten he or she is lying. The same act of supplication, but with the palms facing you, has the opposite interpretation – this person is almost

LEFT Most hand gestures are emotional. This person is clearly friendly and open.

certainly telling you the truth. If someone is hiding the palms from you, he or she is hiding away his or her true self.

Arms crossed over the chest suggest defensiveness; if the hands also grip the arms, there is indignation, and the person's pride has been hurt. If the hands are resting on the arms, the matter can possibly be resolved peacefully; should the hands be fists under the arms, be careful of a temper ready to blow.

When someone raises a hand to his or her throat, he or she is temporarily unsure; this is a good time to press home your point. This gesture, more than any other, tends to precede capitulation in most confrontations, whether they are business, romantic, or social situations. If there is also a slight lowering of the head, you can probably consider the argument already won.

Fiddlers – those who nibble their nails or play with their tie, buttons, or pens and pencils – are the adult equivalent of the thumb-sucking child; they need constant reassurance. Playing with the hair or fingering the collar has a slightly different meaning. If you see someone doing either one, the point is yours for the taking.

LEFT Someone who keeps their hands close to their body is probably introverted or shy.

LEFT If someone is feeling defensive, in an argument for example, they are likely to cross their hands over their chest.

BELOW Fiddlers, like children, need constant reassurance.

FINGER SIGNALS

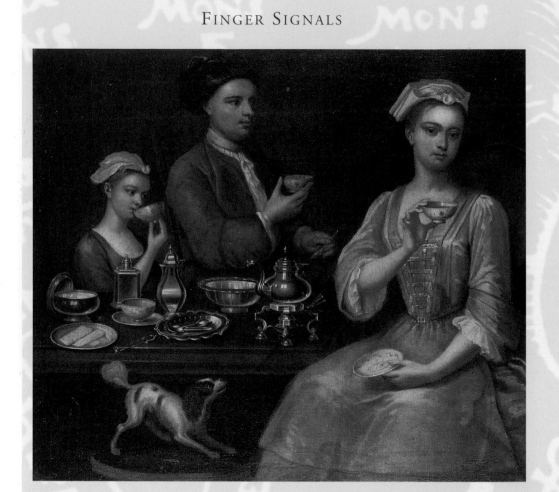

RIGHT The little finger represents independence. Early campaigners for emancipation expressed solidarity by holding out their little fingers when drinking tea.

Fingers are used to convey all sorts of messages, singly or with each other. With the exception of the ring finger (the fourth finger), which cannot always move freely on its own, they all have their own lore and associations.

The first finger, the representation of the ego, is employed for putting others down while emphasizing the self. The middle finger is the most widely used for rude and obscene messages, while the little finger is more often associated with affectation.

Interestingly, the little finger is also used to symbolize independence. Until the middle of the 19th century, women rarely ventured out on their own and had to rely on men to escort them. As British and American women began to campaign for independence and equal voting rights, they banded together. One of the ways they adopted to express their solidarity was to allow their little finger to jut out when drinking a cup of tea; they would also wave to each other in this way.

By crossing our fingers we hope for good luck.

The thumb represents will and authority, and most gestures using the thumb emphasize this in one way or another. The thumbs-down gesture associated with the days of the gladiators of ancient Rome is still used today to express disapproval. In the Western world, pointing with the thumb is the most widely accepted way for a hitchhiker to ask for a ride to their destination. However, in eastern Europe, the Middle East, and Africa, this gesture is anything but acceptable and has negative connotations.

One of the oldest gestures in the world is crossing fingers for good luck. This is a deliberate distortion of the religious three-finger blessing used in the Christian church. It has always been thought unlucky to mimic the actual gesture, so variations on it have been used over the years. If you were to ask people using this gesture whether they were superstitious, most would probably say no. However, were you to see the gesture in a casino overseas, you would be told the person concerned was asking a supervisor if they could take a short break.

The "V" sign, made with the back of the hand facing out, stems from the Middle Ages, when, during battles, captured bowmen might have their first and second fingers cut off. This ensured that even if they escaped alive, they would never be able to use a bow again. Free archers allegedly waved their hands with these two fingers erect as a gesture of defiance and contempt.

The "V" gesture is still used to express similar sentiments in many parts of the world today. This sign is very different from the "V for Victory" sign popularized by Winston Churchill during World War II, and the V "peace sign" used by hippies and antiwar protesters in the 1960s and 1970s. These signs, of course, are made with the palm facing the signer's audience.

LEFT We all keep our fingers crossed for good luck – this is a variation on the Christian three-fingered blessing.

A "thumbs up" sign has different meanings throughout the world.

ABOVE The "thumbs up" may be a signal of approval – but beware that it has negative meaning in the Middle East and Africa.

LEFT Sir Winston Churchill is famous for using the "Victory" sign.

LEFT The "Victory" sign is traditionally a gesture of defiance.

This V sign can mean victory or peace.

Body Language

* * * * * * * * * * * * * * * * * *

LEARNING TO recognize and interpret body language is an art and science in itself which needs to be dealt with in far more depth than would be possible in the following pages. However, it is worth looking at some of the basic concepts and principles just to give some idea of how much can be conveyed by subtle and often unconscious movements, actions, and postures.

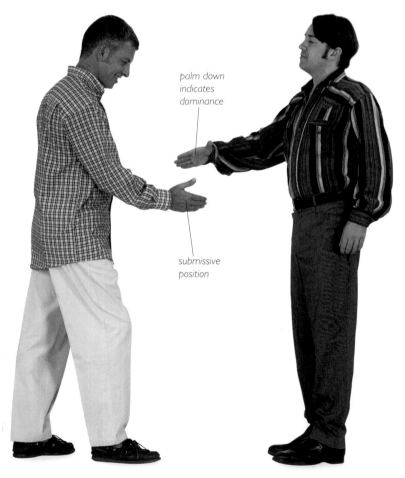

palm down indicates dominance

submissive position

ABOVE When two people meet and shake hands it will be apparent where the balance of power between them lies.

When two people who have not met before approach each other they will signify, by the briefest of pauses or the flicker of an eye, how the scene will continue. One person will adopt a positive stance while the other automatically takes the negative role. The former will stop slightly short of the meeting point to make the latter come to him or her, and he or she may hold out a hand for the other to take.

The hand may be held palm down, the dominant position, which forces the other to turn his or her hand over in a submissive fashion. Then follows what is perhaps the first test of two people's response to one another – the handshake.

Essentially, the handshake is a gesture of peace and goodwill, but the way it is actually done varies enormously. Some people may not offer a hand at all, but will either nod or just give the merest glimpse of a smile. This generally marks a guarded character, someone who may be inwardly unsure. He or she appears to give very little away, but by this deliberate control actually reveals a great deal indeed.

A grip that confuses many people is the one in which the hand is extended slightly curled. This hand is extremely difficult to hold. The other person does not move the hand – you have to shake it. You may console yourself by thinking that you must be superior to this person. Very often, that is exactly what the other person wants you to feel. Such people are usually very clever, able to lead others into a false sense of security. You are dealing with insincerity here, with a person who might possibly be rather emotionally unstable.

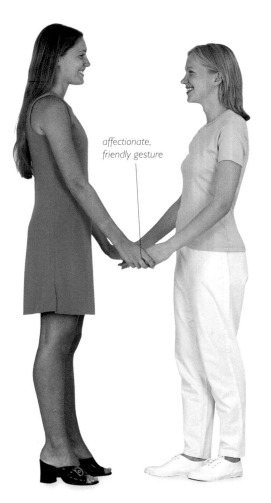

affectionate, friendly gesture

Handshakes tend to differ from country to country, and from culture to culture. People from Latin countries, for example, grip your hand and may embrace you heartily or kiss your cheek. Russians go a stage further – they take your hand, draw you to them and kiss you on the mouth, whatever your sex. Germans, on the other hand, can be very formal and almost theatrical, treating the handshake as an act. There are countless other variations on this almost universal gesture, each one giving some insight into what might be considered cultural values and character.

No matter where the meeting is taking place, once the hands have disengaged, the more dominant person of the two will stand his or her ground. The other has no choice but to step back, accepting the submissive role. No words may have been exchanged yet, but volumes have been spoken. This is the most important part of any meeting. Once the dominant and submissive interplay has been established, it will continue each time these two people communicate.

Elbow pumpers are also disconcerting, for they tend to invade your space without your permission. They grasp your hand in one of theirs, then move in and touch your elbow, upper arm, or shoulder with an intimacy you are not yet ready for. These people feel that they must win you over to their way of thinking – quickly. They will wheedle, twist, and turn, and promise anything because they need to be your friend and must be liked or even loved. However, their promises are false, and given only so that they can get their own way. They actually have very little regard for you; it is only they that matter.

Women tend not to shake hands as much as men, but when they do there is usually more emotion. They frequently take both hands in theirs, which is a strong gesture of intended friendship.

SOCIAL SITUATIONS

Just as we can recognize people by their walk, so we remember some by their gestures and other body movements. Understanding the significance of these gestures and movements can give you a great deal of insight into the people you meet, as well as those you already know – or think you know!

over-firm grip

hand is squeezed

The way someone holds a cigarette or a drink can tell an observer so much. A cigarette held between the middle and third fingers indicates pure affectation. When someone holds a cigarette inside a cupped palm, as if he or she should not be smoking, this suggests a tendency toward secrecy; this person possibly bends the rules and may at times turn out to be slightly untrustworthy.

A glass held by the top with one hand only may indicate an unresolved but temporary problem. If both hands completely cover the base of the glass, the holder probably lives by the motto "Safety first." Those who continually wipe or tap the rim of a glass will try to use others for their own ends.

Some people have such a high degree of self-control that they rarely make any gestures when they socialize. That in itself says much to the trained eye. Once you have learned how to read all the gestures that people make – or do not make – they will speak volumes to you.

A handshake should be firm and last a few seconds. However, some are never forgotten, like the powerhouse handshake. Your hand is gripped, squeezed, pumped violently, and thrown back. This person is basically insecure, a pseudo macho personality who may appear hard, but is plagued by self-doubt.

circling the rim of a wine glass

protecting the neck of the wine glass

INTERVIEWS

folded hands

LEFT An interviewee may be more relaxed if the interviewer sits beside him or her.

Of course, the interviewer's gestures are also significant. A typical opening pose is hands clasped under the chin with the elbows on the desk. This indicates that the interviewee is getting all the attention while he or she is being initially assessed.

ABOVE Although this man may mean well, his closed hands suggest that he is defensive.

Interviews hold terrors for many people, whatever the actual reason for the meeting. Often the interviewer is as nervous as the visitor. But the situation need not be daunting for either one if a few fundamental principles are understood.

It is always helpful for the interviewer to sit with the interviewee, either in two chairs or perhaps on a small sofa, rather than facing him or her across a desk. This will create a more intimate atmosphere that will relax the visitor. The interviewer will obtain better responses, and both people will be able to work together more effectively.

Body language during interviews gives away so much. The interviewee should not cross his or her arms, for this represents defensive aggression. All gestures should be open-handed. A closed hand shows that although the person may mean well, he or she is perhaps not being wholly truthful. Usually, as the interviewee relaxes and opens up, so do his or her gestures.

a closed hand

The table creates a barrier.

The interviewee feels uncomfortable.

When the interviewer sits back in the chair and invites questions, he or she is letting the interviewee know that the session is coming to a close. The interviewee doesn't have much time left in which to make an impression. Any questions he or she asks need to be important ones.

ABOVE Interviews directed across a table may make the interviewee feel hostile.

LEFT A closed hand may mean that the subject is telling a lie or holding back.

PERSONAL ADORNMENT

★ ★ ★ ★ ★ ★ ★ ★ ★ ★ ★ ★ ★ ★ ★ ★ ★

RIGHT Tattooing and body painting has different significances according to culture. This bride wears body paint as part of her wedding ceremony.

HAND READING IS not just about looking at the palm. A good hand analyst also looks at the whole hand and the arm and observes how the subject adorns them with jewelry such as bracelets, rings, or watches. There may be other special features that mark individuality – a tattoo, perhaps, or a scar or other mark.

display to the world; this kind of person has no qualms about attracting attention to themselves.

TATTOOS

Tattoos are very personal adornments and they carry a great deal of meaning in different cultures throughout the world. The image, pattern, and style convey the owner's feelings about the subject of the tattoo. They can take all shapes and sizes and may be very colorful. If the tattoo is in the form of a personal message, it may well have meant more at the time it was done than it does at present.

Also note the location of the tattoo: wrist, forearm and upper arms – even the face – are more likely to be on

RIGHT The degree of tattooing will suggest whether a person is an exhibitionist or not. This Polynesian tribesman displays a decorative yin/yang symbol

WATCHES

Watches can be extremely significant. If the subject is wearing a watch, note its design and condition, how it is positioned, and on which wrist the owner is wearing it.

A watch worn on the left wrist with the face showing suggests that the owner is likely to be fairly average with a conventional outlook. If it's worn face down, or under the wrist, the subject may well have an occupation or leisure interest that could threaten the safety of the timepiece: he or she might be keen on sports, or work in a physically demanding job.

Someone who wears a watch on the right arm is likely to be either left-handed or ambidextrous. They may, however, be affecting a pose. If left-handed, the person will almost certainly have above-average intelligence and a great deal of perception. Remember, left-handed people have learned to live in a right-handed world and to do that they have had to make adjustments and adaptations from a very early age.

Analog watches, which are designed with hands and numerals or marked sections on the outer rim, are often chosen by traditional-minded people.

Those who wear a digital watch probably consider themselves contemporary, modern, and forward looking. They want to know the time the instant they look at their watch without having to work it out.

If there is a calculator attached to the digital watch, the subject probably needs this convenience for his or her use on a regular basis, perhaps for his or her work.

If the watch is of special or unusual design or is obviously expensive, then it can be concluded that the owner either has correspondingly extravagant tastes, or associates with someone close who does.

digital watch
with a
calculator

an elegant
gentleman's
watch

an everyday
watch

BELOW A little detective work can reveal a great deal about an individual. As well as looking at the hands, check to see which kind of watch the subject is wearing.

Rings and Other Jewelry

✶ ✶ ✶ ✶ ✶ ✶ ✶ ✶ ✶ ✶ ✶ ✶ ✶ ✶ ✶ ✶

RINGS AND where they are worn are very informative, although most people aren't aware of some of the deeper significance rings can have.

The lore and language of finger rings have been passed down from the 16th century, when they had very precise meanings. A ring worn on the thumb, for example, signified a physician. General merchants and businessmen wore a ring on their first finger. A ring worn on a man or woman's middle finger was mainly for adornment. A ring on the third finger usually suggested that the wearer was a student or apprentice. Lovers wore rings on their little fingers.

RIGHT The sitter in this 15th-century portrait, is wearing a ring on his thumb. He is known to have been a town clerk in Bavaria, and it is possible that he was a physician as the ring signifies.

RIGHT A young husband puts a marriage ring on his new wife's third finger as part of the Western wedding ceremony.

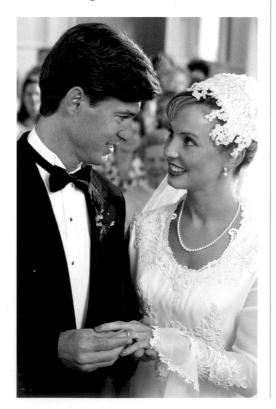

In England, during the reign of George I, wedding rings were usually worn on the thumb, probably because they were fairly heavy and cumbersome. But for countless years, throughout much of the world, wedding rings have been worn on the third finger of the left hand. Traditionally, it was thought a special vein led directly from that digit to the heart. However, in some parts of the world the wedding ring is worn on the third finger of the right hand.

Rings were not always worn on the third phalange as they generally are today. Some people in Western society used to wear rings on the middle phalange, and a special affectation was a ring worn on the nail phalange! It is very rare but not unknown to see a ring worn on one of these phalanges today.

For many years it has been thought by fortune-tellers and medical practitioners alike that a ring emphasized the qualities of the finger upon which it was worn. Thus, a ring on the index finger suggests that the owner is prepared to take the lead, make decisions, and implement them. In practice, people who wear a ring here are often cold-natured, hard, and unforgiving – their heads rule their hearts, and their emotional responses can seem mechanical. They are demanding, unable to relax, and controlling in sexual encounters.

Rings worn on the middle finger show a cool nature, someone who can relax but may always seem a little guarded in dealing with others. These people are probably lonely, perhaps because they've been hurt in the past by a former partner. When you get to know them, it may seem as if they have made a "Ring of Saturn" for themselves.

The third, or annular finger (from the Latin *annularis*, meaning "ring-shaped"), is the most popular ring finger, and a ring worn here implies a good nature, someone who enjoys being in company and probably dislikes being alone for too long.

A ring worn on the Mercury or communication finger almost always conveys a message of some sort. Freemasons wear a ring here, which is often immediately recognized by its unique design. The Freemasons' ring is derived from the late 17th-century "surprise ring," which got its name from a secret hinged surface. It would turn over at a touch to display magical or other designs that revealed either the owner's belief in the magical arts or membership in a secret organization. If of the latter type, the ring's design would have shown the

owner's rank in the group, much as these societies' rings do today.

By the middle of the 19th century, a ring on a woman's little finger signified an independent nature. Women who were involved in the struggle for women's rights are often depicted in paintings of the period with a ring conspicuously worn here. Toward the end of the 20th century, some young people of both sexes who want to emphasize their independence and nonconformity began wearing thumb rings.

People with square hands usually wear rings for a definite purpose. Though they are not true romantics, they may wear a ring as a keepsake to remind them of someone special from the past.

People who have round or conic hands love all kinds of jewelry – the sheer pleasure of wearing nice things always appeals to them. A preference for particularly tasteful, elegant, and esthetically pleasing jewelry is the hallmark of the conic hand.

Spatulate-handed people, who tend to be more physically active, usually do not share these preferences. They might, however, wear rings and jewelry to show off. On special occasions they can sometimes go overboard, bedecking themselves with glittering ornaments that may not always be in the best of taste.

decisive

cool exterior and possible loneliness

good-natured

secretive

LEFT Each ring finger has a different meaning. Don't forget to look at the shape of the hand when considering why the subject is wearing a ring.

NEGATIVE QUALITIES

* * * * * * * * * * * * * * * * * *

BOOKS ON PALMISTRY, astrology, or similar subjects often omit or gloss over the negative qualities these disciplines can reveal. But none of us is perfect, and the hand, as nature's signpost, can point out negative characteristics as well as positive attributes.

It is only fair that we should look at some of these before ending our journey through palmistry.

THE THUMB

If the subject has a negative side to his or her nature, expect to find a weak and poorly formed thumb.

A small, high-set thumb, for example, indicates an idealist, but often one who is emotionally repressed and cannot deal with setbacks. This is a sign of someone who is prepared to take the easy way out of difficulties.

A heavy, low-set thumb suggests a confident streak, but one that may be taken to extremes. Owners of this thumb take risks in order to achieve their aims and may also exhibit unconventional behavior.

A heavy thumb with a bulbous tip, a rarity in itself, shows an incredibly short-fused personality. Their outbursts are often over almost as soon as they start, but by then irreparable damage may have been done.

A thumb with an overdeveloped top phalange also indicates a foul temper, perhaps with occasional streaks of cruelty. If the thumb is large as well, violence may accompany the fits of fury.

Thumb with a bulbous tip – short tempered.

A heavy, low-set thumb – overconfidence.

ABOVE The thumb is a great indicator of character and can pinpoint negative personality traits.

When the top phalange of the thumb turns inward toward the palm, expect to find obstinacy; if the thumb is held close to the fingers, the subject will be tight.

A thumb that bends back at almost a right angle indicates unreliability. People with this type of thumb rarely keep their promises or comply with the terms of an agreement. They were probably sincere when they first committed themselves, but somehow they have found it difficult to keep to their promises and commitments. If the fingertips curl backward or are ultraflexible, this trait may be accentuated. These people are unable to handle money, which slips through their fingers.

No matter what shape or size it is, a thumb that is carried close to the side of the hand shows adherence to convention. There is a lack of independence or will. If the tip points inward toward the palm, there will also be a sense of weakness and inferiority.

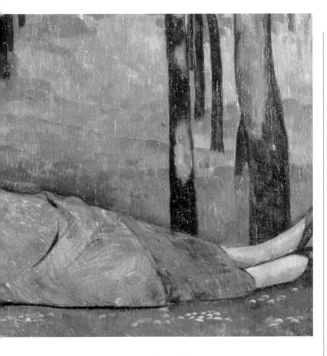

THE FINGERS

If the subject's fingers curl up quickly but open slowly, he or she may be a tightwad – but look for other signs elsewhere in the hand to confirm this, as this action may be the result of physical problems such as arthritis or rheumatism.

When the base phalange of each finger is puffy, there is a love of food and drink, but little concern for diet. The subject is also likely to have crude table manners.

An overlong bottom phalange on the middle finger in comparison with the base phalanges of the other fingers on the same hand can reveal miserly traits.

People who have crooked fingers can be untrustworthy and inclined to self-deceit. An exceptionally long Mercury finger suggests a hypocritical nature. People with this configuration are not particularly truthful and are likely to use others for their own purposes without conscience.

A very long, strong, and straight first finger indicates a strong ego; such people are often vain, controlling, and domineering. If the palm is soft to the touch there may be some cruelty as well.

Long, tapering fingers belong to sensitive dreamers. This in itself is not necessarily a negative trait, but it can lead to difficult behavior. For example, procrastination can be second nature for these people. They may be inherently lazy and only manage to give lip service to their obligations.

People with nails broader than they are long are argumentative. Very large, square nails show a cold, selfish inner nature. Short nails suggest a quick temper and a highly critical nature. Such people are likely to lecture and harangue others, sometimes almost endlessly. The more flesh there is between the end of a nail and a fingertip, the more explosive the temper, especially with a bitten nail. It doesn't take much to start these people off, but it takes a lot to stop them once they have begun.

LEFT A dreamer will have long tapering fingers; it will take work to bring these people back to earth.

LEFT Nail-biting is nearly always a sign of nervous energy and inner tension.

The Palm and the Mounts

* * * * * * * * * * * * * * * *

overdeveloped
mount of Saturn

flat mount
of Jupiter

high mount
of Apollo

overdeveloped
zone of Mars

fleshy Venus
mount

high Luna mount

RIGHT Negative qualities will show in a variety of ways on the palmar mounts.

ABOVE Criminal behavior cannot always be predicted by hand reading, but it will probably be confirmed in the individual's hand.

PEOPLE WITH thick palms generally lack consideration for others. They are selfish, and are often oblivious to the needs of more sensitive people.

An overdeveloped mount of Venus indicates that the subject's sensual side is dominant, often accompanied by a selfish, hedonistic approach. Should this mount be flat and underdeveloped, the inner nature is cold and rather lifeless.

A Jupiter mount that is overdeveloped and inclines toward the Saturn mount suggests a domineering nature with a good deal of personal conceit. This is the type of person who goes to extremes to get his or her own way. People who marry for money or status rather than love are likely to have this configuration. To make matters worse, this sort of person will not hesitate to drop a current love if someone wealthier or more influential arrives on the scene.

An absent, or flat, mount of Jupiter implies a lazy nature, someone who has little or no active ambition. Punctuality is not this person's forte.

A very high Apollo mount shows an unstable and untruthful type. Hypocrisy, trickery, and deception are likely, especially if the Mercury mount is developed but the finger is short.

When the zone of Mars is well developed the owner may have an excess of misplaced energy. He or she has a rebellious nature. If challenged, the subject will be defensive and defiant. Such people often exaggerate.

An underdeveloped area here suggests a lack of courage or moral fiber. These people are unable to fight for what is theirs and will back away from confrontation.

A high Luna mount indicates a fertile imagination. Such people find it hard to maintain personal discipline.

CRIME IN THE HAND

No one line or collection of lines can, in and of itself, indicate whether the owner is a law-abiding person. Nor does the shape of a hand imply criminality. But once a criminal has been positively identified, the shape of the hand, combinations of lines, and certain hand gestures can sometimes shed light on why he or she may have strayed and turned to crime.

Often, people are likely to turn to some form of criminal behavior because of envy or jealousy coupled with low self-esteem. When the index finger is shorter than the third and leans quite definitely toward the middle finger, the owner lacks pride in himself or herself. These people frequently consider themselves unable to improve their lot. They feel they have reached the limit of their capabilities and have resigned themselves to their fate. This is especially so if the head and heart lines are joined together, always the sign of very low self-confidence coupled with poor self-esteem in the early years.

A short middle finger always indicates someone who is prepared to gamble to get what he or she wants. This may be just a weakness in some people, but in others it can become almost an illness.

Such people seem to have an unwavering optimism that everything will be all right if they can only win "the big one." To this end they will gamble absolutely anything and everything, without a thought to the consequences of what they might stand to lose – generally speaking, the possibility doesn't even enter their mind. Naturally, debts soon mount up and some people eventually turn to crime to recoup some of their losses.

Check the index finger.

Check the head and heart lines.

LEFT Crime may show in the hands; a fused head and heart line is a sign of low self-confidence and a short Apollo finger would suggest a lack of self-appreciation.

BELOW LEFT The criminal may have low self-esteem as indicated by a short index finger.

BELOW A short Saturn finger belongs to those who will take any risk to get what they want. This type is probably a gambler.

CRIMINAL TYPES

✶ ✶ ✶ ✶ ✶ ✶ ✶ ✶ ✶ ✶ ✶ ✶ ✶ ✶ ✶ ✶

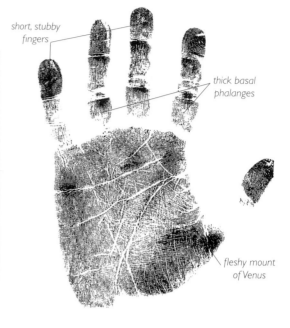

short, stubby fingers

thick basal phalanges

fleshy mount of Venus

CRIMINOLOGISTS AND psychiatrists are generally in agreement that there are five main categories of lawbreaker: the instinctive type, the impulsive type, the habitual type, the passionate type, and the criminally insane type. Whichever category they fall into, those who turn to crime must be regarded as somehow unstable and, in a sense, therefore, morally, mentally, or emotionally unsound.

Instinctive lawbreakers are opportunists. Led by uncontrolled drives, they may, on impulse, take some but not all the money from a purse, yet no one would dream that they were culpable. They are usually more likely to offend against morals or property than against people. People with round or conic hands are perhaps more prone to such temptations than those with square or rectangular palms. This of course does not mean that everyone with round or conic hands is likely to break the law, but if they do stray it is more likely to be in an instinctive or impulsive way.

The habitual type is spurred on by the sheer excitement of criminal behavior – these types of people do not seem to understand that one day they might get caught. It is unusual for them to offend against people, and jealousy and envy are usually the driving forces when they steal or damage property. In these cases the hands are likely to be soft to the touch, which reflects a lack of drive and personal initiative.

RIGHT The hand-print of Charles Manson who was responsible for a mass murder in the United States. Note the hump in the head line suggesting distorted thinking.

BELOW Scarface of gangster law, was probably a habitual criminal; for the gangster crime is a way of life.

The impulsive criminal seizes the sudden opportunity that comes out of the blue. Suddenly blind to all reason, he or she just strikes while the iron is hot and usually lives to regret it for the rest of his or her life. The impulsive hand may be square, round, or spatulate with a long palm and short, stubby, "mixed" fingers. Once again, the palm is soft to the touch; it usually has many small lines crisscrossing it.

Passionate types are driven by possessiveness. They usually come from a "good" environment, but want more of whatever it is that drives them to commit their crimes. These characters are more likely to offend against other people than property, unless they can get at the people they want to hurt by destroying their property. Once again, the conic or spatulate hand is most common here, especially those with short mixed fingers, for these people are most susceptible to the mood of the moment. They seize an opportunity when they see it, and they act on it immediately.

Finally, the criminally insane often appear and act normal until they are confronted. They may plan their acts down to the last detail, or they may simply go off the rails in one crazed moment. Their most likely target is other people.

It is difficult to characterize the hands of this last type. Years of studying the hands of killers have revealed no discernible pattern. One particularly nasty killer, for example, had hands with almost nothing to indicate criminal behavior or the way his killings were carried out. He had very square palms with long, straight, square fingers, indicating excessive zeal for doing things with the utmost attention to detail. Actually, it was this very attention to detail that brought about his eventual downfall.

In fact, people with square hands, especially when the hand is firm to the touch, are the most likely to respect law, order, and discipline. Often, our guardians of the law – police officers, prison guards, and peacekeepers – tend to have rectangular

ABOVE Those who fight crime are likely to have square hands.

or square hands. There is frequently a very good fate line clearly marked from the wrist to the top of the hand in this type of person. The presence of a fate line usually signifies a sense of responsibility and ambition.

Please remember, none of the negative indications should be construed as definite character failings or weaknesses present within the personality. However, those who do have hand configurations as described and who do find themselves prone to temptation may be inclined to act or react as stated by the hand reader.

ABOVE The print of a policeman, showing a good fate line on a rectangular hand.

LEFT Each of the three hands – taken from an old manuscript – contain negative but very different qualities. All were murderers.

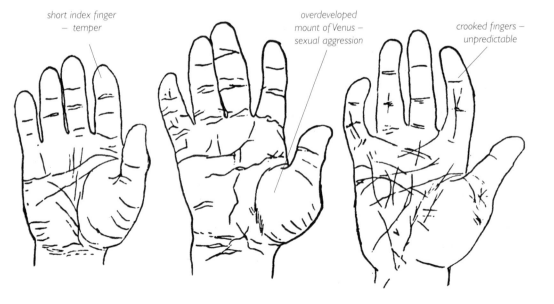

short index finger – temper

overdeveloped mount of Venus – sexual aggression

crooked fingers – unpredictable

PALMISTRY AND ASTROLOGY

★ ★ ★ ★ ★ ★ ★ ★ ★ ★ ★ ★ ★ ★ ★ ★

THERE IS a provable relationship between palmistry and astrology, but while the interpretations and meanings of the individual planets are similar, the two disciplines employ different approaches. With astrology, for example, complex mathematical procedures are used to set up a birth chart that then must be interpreted. In palmistry, however, the hand is held open for examination, ready for instant analysis. But both disciplines offer surprising levels of accuracy.

RIGHT An illustration of a birth chart from Robert Fludd's writings on astrology (1617–1624).

The arrangement of the planets on the fingers and palmar surface has remained fairly constant since the Middle Ages. However, there are slight differences as to location on the hand.

In the first system we are going to look at, the sign of Aries is placed at the end of the life line, on the mount of Neptune. Many modern palmistry experts, however, favor placing Aries at the start of the life line – Aries, after all, is the first point of the zodiac and coincides with the start of spring and new life. Taurus corresponds with the mount of Venus, the seat of life; in astrology Taurus is ruled by Venus. Gemini is placed at the base of the Jupiter mount, toward the accepted traditional start of the life line. These three signs represent spring and are located in the area of the palm we most associate with happiness, pleasure, and general well-being. More to the point, it is the area from where all life begins.

ABOVE The star sign Leo represents pride, authority, and royalty.

The summer signs are Cancer, Leo, and Virgo, and when these signs take prominence each year we are usually at our most active. Furthermore, these signs, placed as they are on the first finger, imply that we will follow our ambitions with honor and integrity.

Autumn is indicated by Libra, Scorpio, and Sagittarius, which are found on the Apollo finger. The implication is quite clear. We set out to enjoy the fruits of our success with wisdom in an honorable manner.

The winter period in astrology is represented by the astrological signs of Capricorn, Aquarius, and Pisces. Capricorn is placed on the lower part of the Apollo mount, and Aquarius is situated on the upper part of the Luna mount.

Pisces takes up its position on the lower part of the Luna mount. We may interpret this as living our old age with the dignity and maturity that come with the multitude of experiences that life sends our way.

The most widely used system in modern times also stems from the Middle Ages, and places the signs of the zodiac on the phalanges of each finger. In the Middle Ages, it was believed that the palm represented the source of life, and the development of the fingers indicated the individual's progress. In line with this thinking, some hand analysts today associate hand shapes with the astrological elements or triplicities; fire, earth, air and water.

The Fire hand has a long palm and short fingers. The main lines are strongly etched and fairly plentiful, although this is not quite considered a "full" hand.

The Earth hand is represented by a square palm with short fingers and few lines on the palmar surface; it is really closer to what is called the "empty" hand. There may, however, be traces of some rather weak-looking lines here and there.

The Air hand is fleshy, with a square palm and long, flexible fingers. Generally, there should be an average distribution of palmar lines, both major and minor, possibly leaning toward the "full" hand.

The Water hand has a long palm and long fingers. It may be slightly delicate in appearance, with a palm full of lines that crisscross in all directions, none very strong.

By referring to the fundamental astrological interpretations of the four types, we can create a basic personality profile for each hand type.

People with Air hands are adaptable, though not necessarily practical but inclined more toward the intellectual. This corresponds approximately with the air signs, Gemini, Libra, and Aquarius.

Those with Water hands always have emotional overtones to their actions and reactions. They are impressionable, creative, and often very intuitive. These characteristics match those of Cancer, Scorpio, and Pisces.

The Earth hand indicates a largely practical approach to life. These people are physically active and have orderly minds.

This description applies equally well to Taurus, Virgo, and Capricorn.

The Fire hand suggests energy with a positive and ardent nature full of vitality; a good portrayal of Aries, Leo, and Sagittarius.

To correlate between palmistry and astrology, make good-quality handprints and draw up the birth chart, or have one drawn up for you. Study and analyze both sets of information very carefully. Then draw a line down the middle of a sheet of paper, and begin listing the most obvious features you find from each discipline. As you do so, you should start to see a striking similarity between the two lists. This presupposes that you can perform equally well in both disciplines. If not, select the discipline with which you feel most comfortable and ask a friend who works well in the alternative one to do the basic work for you. As you progress, you will each begin to find two sets of information that are remarkably alike.

For example, a conic hand with a good creative curve, with fingers about the same length as the palm and evenly spaced, suggests an open, friendly, artistic, creative type. Astrologically, this may be shown by the sun in Gemini with the moon in Leo.

A palm covered with many fine lines, a "full" hand, suggests a vivid imagination and a mind that is rarely still – characteristics you'd be likely to find in someone with the moon in Gemini and Mercury in Cancer.

These examples are meant as guides only. Practice is always the only way to achieve any level of ability.

ABOVE Aries, the ram, is the first sign of the zodiac and is associated with spring. It correlates with the start of the life line on the palm.

LEFT The moon is ruler of the planets and it is associated with the feminine principle and the subconscious in astrology.

ABOVE The characteristics of Cancer are often found in those who have Water hands.

PALMISTRY AND GRAPHOLOGY

* * * * * * * * * * * * * * * * *

THERE IS a close relationship between palmistry and graphology – perhaps not surprising, since the two disciplines are so directly concerned with the hand. In a great many cases, the shapes and patterns of a person's hand are reflected in his or her handwriting. Using the guidelines that follow, you should be able to picture your subject with a little extra accuracy by studying a handwriting sample.

People who write in a basically upright style often have square hands. The palm is firm to the touch, with well-spaced fingers. A well-balanced thumb should be present to support this. The first finger will be the same length or just a shade longer than the third finger. If the writing is firm with heavy pressure, the first finger probably will be slightly longer. (To check for heavy pressure, turn the paper over and hold it up to the light. You will be able to see definite trace marks of the script. The clearer the outline, the heavier the pressure.) With heavy pressure, the hand will feel firm, and the line of life will be strongly marked. The other major lines will probably be heavily etched as well. Those who demonstrate passionate moods or who get carried away with the mood of the moment may have a partly or wholly formed Sydney line or Simian line. (See pages 58 and 91.)

When the handwriting has a backward slope, the lines of head and life are likely to be joined at the start. Should the script also be rounded, both lines will stay joined together for some way into the palm. The hand is likely to be "full," with many lines crisscrossing the palmar surface.

ABOVE People with square hands will have an upright writing style.

RIGHT Different styles of writing will correlate to characteristics that are suggested in the hands.

Forward-slanting writing indicates sociability, probably accompanied by an impulsive nature. The hand will have long palms and short fingers.

When the writing slants very far forward and has many loops, the palm will be soft to the touch. There may also be a long, sloping head line, possibly frayed or "furry" at about the point of the subject's current age.

Large handwriting looks confident and striking when it splashes across a page, but if it is too large it can seem immature, or even childish. Excessively large or small handwriting can indicate other problems.

In general, large writing indicates expansiveness with poor self-control but a strong desire to be noticed. The writer wants

large, confident handwriting

backward, sloping handwriting

to be at the center of everything. The hands will be soft and conic, or round, with fleshy basal phalanges. An overdeveloped mount of Jupiter with a full Luna mount are also likely; both may be soft to the touch.

When handwriting is very small the writer often suffers from inner tension. These people are likely to be neat, possibly to an excessive degree. Restlessness is another possibility. Writers like this are likely to have small, thin fingers and palms with signs of inner tension. There may be longitudinal fluting on the nails, and influence lines entering the Luna mount at the percussion; both of these traits also suggest restlessness.

Where handwriting is so tiny that it is nearly illegible, the hand will also show signs of deliberate deceitfulness. The little finger will be small or poorly formed, with an overdeveloped mount.

If there is a backward slope to the script, the thumbs will oppose the fingers when relaxed. These writers often present an outward persona very different from their real "inner" self.

Handwriting with a mixed slant and a wavy baseline implies poor self-control. There may be many reasons for this. Some writers, for example, may have such a quick perception rate that their hand cannot keep up with the sheer speed with which their mind processes information. People like this may start tasks hesitantly, especially if pressured by stronger personalities. Here there would be a soft spatulate or "flared" hand with mixed fingers shorter than the palm. The third finger will be longer than the first. The head line will be wavy, probably islanded or chained in places. Dots, bars, and influence lines will also be found along the line. All these features indicate inner tension. If there is a fate line it is likely to be short, badly broken, or weak looking.

Handwriting with medium pressure, a good "rhythm," and reasonably well-dotted i's and fairly well-crossed t's is a sign of a good memory with a sound, commonsense approach to life. In this case the hand will be firm, with a well-formed thumb. On the palmar surface, the heart and head lines are likely to run parallel, and the more even the "quadrangle" seems, the more common sense the owner displays.

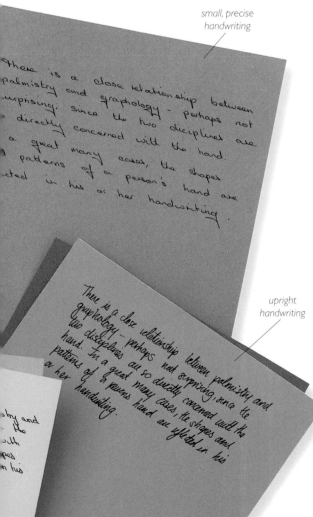

ABOVE If the subject's handwriting splashes over the page, look for a conic hand with fleshy basal phalanges. These people need lots of attention.

small, precise handwriting

upright handwriting

171

PALMISTRY AND THE TAROT

* * * * * * * * * * * * * * * *

IT DOES not take long to discover the relationship between Tarot, that most occult of all the ancient art/sciences, and astrology. And the deeper we look, the more we find – there are correspondences with the seasons, the months of the year, the constellations, and so much more. Since we have already noted the correspondences between astrology and palmistry, it follows logically that there are connections between palmistry and the Tarot as well.

In the Tarot, the first Arcanum (or card number 1), the Magician or Juggler, corresponds with the top phalange of the thumb. This card symbolizes the person who directs his or her will with a positive force. Similarly, in palmistry, the first phalange of the thumb represents directed will.

The second phalange of the thumb is where we look to discover a subject's reason and logic, and this is where we place the second Arcanum, the High Priestess. This card (number 2) represents occult science, the origin of all the later sciences.

The third Arcanum, the Empress, symbolizes emotion in action as represented by our mundane passions. On the hand, the mount of Venus is where we would assess the level of our emotions in action.

The next three Arcana, the Emperor, the Pope, and the Lovers, correlate with the Jupiter finger. In palmistry, this finger and its mount represent leadership, ambition, and our religious convictions. The Emperor corresponds with the first phalange, for both are concerned with worldly power; the Pope equates with the second phalange, showing spiritual

ABOVE The Pope correlates with the Jupiter finger to signify religious conviction.

ABOVE The Emperor correlates with the Jupiter finger to denote ambition.

Jupiter finger

LEFT The High Priestess correlates with the second phalange of the thumb to signify logic.

LEFT The Magician corresponds with the tip of the thumb to signify willpower.

ABOVE Lovers compare with the third phalange of the Jupiter finger to signify harmony.

ABOVE The Chariot, depicting a man being pulled between the active and the passive, corresponds with the top of the Saturn finger.

RIGHT Justice correlates with the middle phalange of the Saturn finger.

Saturn finger

awareness. The Lovers compare with the third phalange, for they both indicate how well spiritual and worldly qualities harmonize within us.

The middle, or Saturn finger, is the finger of balance. In the Tarot, the Chariot, Justice, and the Hermit correspond respectively with each of this finger's phalanges. This finger indicates how we might maintain a natural balance in all we do. It is a sign of how we care, of our caution and our maturity. The finger position is perfect, placed between Jupiter signifying ambition, and Apollo signifying brilliance and dash.

It is often suggested that the Chariot depicts man being pulled between active and passive forces. To establish a true harmony between them we must establish a proper balance, as shown by the card that represents Justice. The Hermit indicates caution, prudence, and wisdom. In palmistry this is indicated by the bottom phalange of the middle finger and the mount of Saturn.

ABOVE The second phalange of the Jupiter finger represents religious convictions and spiritual awareness.

LEFT The Hermit, like the basal phalange of Saturn, denotes caution and wisdom.

ABOVE The Wheel of Fortune is represented in the Apollo finger to show realism and practicality as part of the character.

The Wheel of Fortune, Force, and the Hanged Man can be seen in the Apollo finger, which in palmistry represents the person's artistic and creative side. If this finger is very long, it suggests a gambling nature, or someone who is in search of the pleasures of life.

Card number ten, the Wheel of Fortune, complements the Apollo finger's first phalange. The middle phalange shows our realism and practicality, corresponding with the strength of character shown by card number 11, Force. The third phalange correlates with the symbolism of card number 12, the Hanged Man, which sends warnings of dire consequences unless the right thing is done at the right time.

Cards 13, 14, and 15 – Death, Temperance, and the Devil – correspond with the Mercury finger and mount. An overdeveloped or badly formed finger and mount of Mercury can imply criminal tendencies, just as Tarot card number 13 warns that unless there is a change in the lower nature, the subject will suffer serious consequences. There must be harmony between the lower and higher natures as shown by card number 14, Temperance.

Overdevelopment of the lower phalange of this finger is a sure indication that the baser Mercurial qualities are prominent and affect the subject's character. He or she, therefore, could be in considerable danger of spiritual destruction, as

BELOW The third phalange of the Apollo finger is represented by the Hanged Man in Tarot.

ABOVE Force, shown here beating a hog, is equivalent to the Apollo finger which represents creative energies in the subject.

symbolized by card number 15, the Black Magician, or the Devil.

The next three Arcana – the Tower of Destruction, the Star, and the Moon – all find correspondences on the Luna mount. A strongly developed mount can make a person dream too much, putting him or her in danger of becoming muddled and impractical. Imagination without proper control leads to trouble – the subject can be the root of his or her own downfall. People like this are capable of destroying themselves through selfishness only they can cure.

Arcana number 16 is the lightning-struck Tower, a card that represents self-destruction. However, people can find their niche through their dreams, which in turn will give inner peace and harmony, provided goals are pursued with the hope that all will go well. The Star, card number 17, is the symbol of that hope.

But there are still hidden dangers lurking if these ambitions are carried too far. There has to be a solid foundation for all these aspirations, for although the Moon (card number 18) indicates any hidden problems, it only reflects them.

The next three cards, numbers 19, 20, and 21 – the Sun, Judgment, and the World – correspond with the zone of Mars, which includes both of the mounts of Mars. This zone is a very important area of the hand, for it is where our everyday struggles are clearly

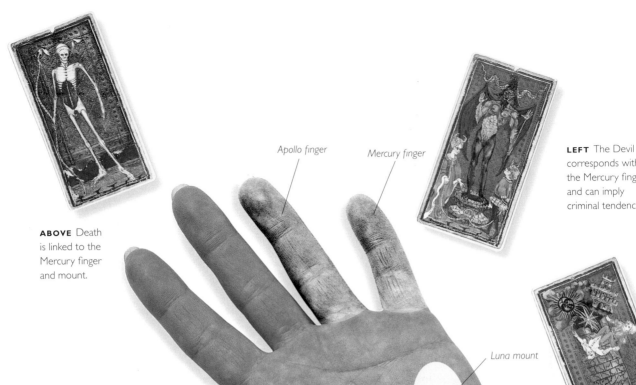

Apollo finger

Mercury finger

Luna mount

ABOVE Death is linked to the Mercury finger and mount.

LEFT Temperance corresponds to balance between phalanges in the Mercury finger.

LEFT The Devil corresponds with the Mercury finger and can imply criminal tendencies.

ABOVE The Tower of Destruction – signifying self-destruction – can be associated with the Luna mount.

marked. Here we assess the development of our mundane qualities, such as material happiness. In this zone we note the fortitude we have when confronting adversity and record our coolness or daring.

The Tarot is perfectly represented in this area: the Sun corresponds with material happiness; Judgment symbolizes decisions and actions in response to problems; and the World shows how we cope with the results.

The final arcanum, number 22, the Fool, corresponds with the hand as a whole. It tells us that we should not take anything for granted. Rather, we must evaluate everything according to the power we have, or think we have, as it is reflected in our hand. Thus, from the hand, as in the Tarot, we can learn our path in life. The Fool may be interpreted as man progressing to perfection by treading the path he recognizes, keeping the courage to continue until he succeeds.

There are many versions of Tarot packs, and far more variations when it comes to their interpretation. Purists should try to remember this when they experiment with the above correspondences.

ABOVE The Fool denotes spontaneity, trust, and risk-taking in Tarot.

PALMISTRY AND NUMEROLOGY

* * * * * * * * * * * * * * * *

THE CORRESPONDENCES between numerology and palmistry are somewhat similar to those between astrology and palmistry. However, there are no nuances or subtlety in numerology.

For the beginner, numerology is more straightforward and easier to understand than other disciplines; it is also more directly concerned with character and personality. In addition, when it comes to timing events, it can help pinpoint incidents with surprising accuracy.

In numerology, each letter of the alphabet is assigned a number from 1 to 26; to obtain the final value of each letter, double figures must be reduced to a single digit. For example, the 12th letter, L, has a final value of 3 (1+2).

The following paragraphs give a very brief interpretation of the characteristics associated with each of the nine numbers, followed by a description of what one might expect to find in a hand corresponding with the numerological description given. Not all the features will be present in every case, but at least some of them are likely to be found.

ABOVE
Numerology is an easy discipline for beginners to learn about and relate to palmistry.

NUMBER 1

These people dislike bureaucracy and restraint and often speak their minds. Natural leaders, they don't quite fit into a set pattern, yet they can become set in their ways fairly early in life. They not only plan well, they expect their plans to come to fruition quickly; they dislike delay. They need to exercise more tolerance, for they generally tend to judge others by their own standards.

ANALYZING A NAME

Here are the values for the alphabet in full:

1	A	J	S
2	B	K	T
3	C	L	U
4	D	M	V
5	E	N	W
6	F	O	X
7	G	P	Y
8	H	Q	Z
9	I	R	

To analyze a name, simply add up the values of the letters and reduce the total until you arrive at a single digit. For example:

PETER WEST
7+5+2+5+9+5+5+1+2=41;
4 + 1 = 5

Thus, the name reduces to and equals 5.

To arrive at the number for your name, always use the name by which you are most widely known – Peter, for example, is often shortened to "Pete".

To determine a birth number, simply add up the numbers of the birth date and reduce them to a single digit.
For example, Peter was born on June 24, 1939, which makes the birth number 7.

(6+2+4+1+9+3+9=34;
3+4=7)

Adding the name number to the birth number yields a third and equally significant number, often referred to as the Destiny number, in this case 12 or 1 + 2 = 3.

This gives a choice of three numbers to assess and interpret. The result will reveal many personal characteristics of the subject. (A repeated number enhances its value and its meaning even further.)

Expect to find a dominant first and middle finger, with a wide space between all the fingers. The thumb would be wide-angled but well balanced in relation to the other fingers. The palm would be broad and the wrist thick. There would be few lines, and what lines there are would be strongly marked. The basal phalanges of the fingers might be slightly overdeveloped.

NUMBER 2

This type of person prefers to work quietly in the background, for he or she loves peace and harmony. Gentle and courteous, these people get easily depressed if things go wrong. They lack resilience, and may also lack self-confidence. Despite all this, they do have a way of working with others, and are often found as the "power behind the throne." In business, they can be excellent as the second in command.

These people might have small hands with narrow, soft, squarish palms and fingers of equal length. The thumb might have a long second phalange, suggesting diplomacy. Their skin pattern would be "closed" or fine, perhaps with loops on each fingertip.

NUMBER 3

These people prefer to keep moving. They are ambitious and never really satisfied by routine work. Variety attracts them, in both work and leisure pursuits. Conscientious and practical, they can worry themselves silly over trivia if things are not quite right, for order and discipline are their forte. With their natural charm and sense of humor, they make wonderful hosts.

A wide, conic palm with a "full" hand and flexible fingers is suggested here. The thumb might also be flexible. Nails may be short, and a couple of them might possibly be bitten. The fingers would be short in relation to the palm.

NUMBER 4

Independent, sensitive, loyal, but a little rebellious at times, these people are easily hurt by the wrong word or deed. Either they are conservative in their habits or dress, or they are completely the opposite. They do better as part of a team than on their own. They often dream of getting away from it all, but rarely put their plans into action. Practical, persevering, and hard-working, reliability is their strength.

Almost the classic square palm is implied here. This is the typical Earth hand, but modified with a long, sensitive head line that may have an island or two or perhaps some chaining. The thumb would not be overlong or strong but would oppose the fingers when held in a relaxed position.

ABOVE Number three people enjoy hosting parties and have natural flair.

LEFT Chance and the random fall of numbers plays an important part in numerology.

NUMBER 5

These people will try anything once, just for the experience. Versatile, quick, open, and friendly, they have a wide circle of friends and acquaintances, often including social leaders. They are often known for their honesty. Money, however, tends to pass through their hands. Changeable and restless, they are impossible to reform.

Expect to find short conic hands and fingers, soft to the touch. The thumbs would be yielding and flexible. The first and fourth fingers are likely to stand away from their neighbors. The head and heart lines may be forked, and the life line would end on the Luna mount. There may also be well-padded Jupiter and Apollo mounts.

NUMBER 6

These people can be rather sentimental and quiet, but with a happy talent for making and keeping friends. Expect to find a natural personal magnetism with a refined manner. Extremely stubborn, these people love and hate with equal intensity. Some seem to prefer solitude, often a kind of martyrdom.

There may be smooth fingers on soft conic palms, and a sensitive heart line sweeping well down into the palm. The head line would be firm. There might be one or two sensitivity pads on the fingers, and the middle finger might be overlong. The thumb would be large, stiff,

BELOW The number six denotes the affectionate type, although they may be sentimental.

and unyielding, opposing the fingers. The wrist would be thick where it joins the hand.

NUMBER 7

Fond of occult matters and difficult to get to know properly, these people have little time for ordinary rules and regulations. They must have total freedom and independence at all times, and they live by their own principles, which may be hard for others to define or understand. Restless, they have a great love of travel. They are noted for their loyalty, honesty, and commitment.

The subject would have a "full" hand with a good line of intuition. The head line would be long and widely forked at the end, and there would be many short influence lines entering the palm from the percussion on the lower part of the Luna mount. The fingers would be mixed, with a long medius, knotted at both phalanges. The fingerprints would display whorl-type patterns.

NUMBER 8

These people can be ruthless, hard, and practical, rather like a machine. They are achievers and survivors who work and play with equal intensity. They won't hurt anyone else unless they are hurt. Fatalistic, they find it difficult to adapt: they prefer the tried and trusted and are strongly resistant to anything new. They will have many acquaintances but few really trusted friends.

Expect to find square hands and fingers with a long, clearly etched fate line to the base of the middle finger. On the right hand there would be a high-set heart line or a broken simian line. The fingers and thumbs would be stiff, the zone of Mars well developed. Overall, there would be relatively few lines, perhaps an "empty" hand. The head and life lines might be separated at the beginning, but would perhaps have slight hairlines between them.

NUMBER 9

These people display an inborn desire for leadership, perhaps more for the power it confers. Generally constructive, honest, and solid, they may be overcritical, but find it difficult to accept criticism themselves. They have a vigorous air about them, and cannot sit still for long. Hard to live with, they pursue the mood and fancy of the moment and zealously preserve their freedom. They have an ability to reverse disadvantages by the sheer force of their personality.

These subjects would have large, wide hands, either rectangular or firm and conic, with a well-developed base and with the principal lines strongly marked. There would be long, flexible first and second fingers, with knots at both joints and high mounts. The thumb would be large and wide-angled.

Astrology, graphology, Tarot, and numerology are among the most widely used systems in character and personality assessment. The relationships demonstrated here may also be adapted to find correlations between any of the four disciplines. All the basic ideas are here. The way is now open for you to experiment with all your newfound knowledge. Practice on yourself first. Through palmistry, you can learn what your strengths and weaknesses are, and where your talents really lie, so that you can make good career moves when the time is right. You can monitor your health so that you can be sure of having the stamina you need for any testing times you may have to face. And you can improve existing relationships in all areas of your life, and ensure that new relationships are successful. With good powers of observation, you can even learn to assess other people, almost anywhere and at any time, usually without them being aware of it.

For most people, learning how to live and get along with other people starts at home, in childhood. Therefore we will start with early childhood experiences and move through to adulthood, exploring several important facets of life along the way.

LEFT Smooth fingers with soft, conic palms relate to the number six. They may be overly sentimental.

AFTERWORD

★ ★ ★ ★ ★ ★ ★ ★ ★ ★ ★ ★ ★ ★ ★ ★

To ACHIEVE PROFICIENCY at anything, you need to do more than just read a book and put it back on the shelf. Regular practice is essential. Fortunately, there are many opportunities every day to practice hand reading in a useful way.

For example, if, first thing in the morning, you feel a little off-color, and think you'd better go back to bed for a few more hours, test the "mouse," the health mount at the back of the thumb and first finger. If the mounts on both hands are firm, the off-color feeling is only temporary. If, however, they are flat and lifeless, you really are below par and may need to seek medical advice.

The "mouse" or health mount

ABOVE Test the firmness of the health mount if you are feeling unwell.

ABOVE Those who crowd fellow passengers are likely to have thick basal phalanges.

Look at your fingertips. If there are "white lines" on the top phalanges, then you really are tired and run down. Try to adjust your day and accommodate this so that you can get more rest.

If your nails are pale or even slightly bluish, you need to get some fresh air into your lungs. If there are any horizontal ridges across your nails, especially the thumbnails, you may be slightly stressed. Longitudinal ridging may indicate worry and tension – if you know the cause, you can make definite steps to ease the problem.

When you step out of the front door, learn to observe the people with whom you come into contact, albeit fleetingly. Public transportation can be a mine of information if you just take the time to look at the hands of all those strangers around you.

LEFT This enchanting picture called *The Palms Foretell* was painted by William Roberts (1895–1980).

Notice how people travel. Look out for the "space invaders," those people who take up far more room than they should and are unwilling to move over when the bus or train gets crowded. The basal phalanges of each of their fingers will probably be puffy, indicating their selfishness.

If the person opposite you seems attractive, take some time to look at his or her hands and see what you can find out. Notice if he or she is wearing a ring, and on which finger. (If nothing else, this should tell you whether the person is married!) Is there a watch? How is the person wearing it? Does he or she appear to "pose" with a pen, or hold a newspaper or book in an unusual way? With some observation, using all your powers of discretion of course, you can discover a great deal. Of course, any assessment of this sort has to be one-sided; however the art of covert observation can be a lot of fun!

Perhaps there's a difficult interview ahead of you later in the day. If you remember how to sit and keep your gestures positive, you'll have very little to worry about. If you are conducting the interview, observe the interviewee's hands and gestures to help you refine your assessment of him or her.

By observing hands and gestures, extraordinary progress can be made in all walks of life. Teachers find they can gain valuable insights into some of their students, or salesmen may be able to close a deal successfully with previously problematic customers. You will soon find that time spent observing hands will almost always prove productive.

It may not be easy at first, but you will get steadily better with plenty of practice.

Everything you need to know is in this book. Any of the situations described can be adjusted and adapted to meet your own particular needs. At the very least, using palmistry will give you an edge that you did not hitherto have – and any advantage is better than none.

LEFT You can check out prospective partners with a good look at their hands on your first date!

BELOW The tradition of fortune telling and palm reading has a long history and continues to grow in popularity.

BELOW Being observant can be of great advantage. If you are attracted to somebody, you'll be able to tell by the ring on the third finger if they are married or not.

GLOSSARY

* * * * * * * * * * * * * * * * * *

OVER THE YEARS palmistry has undergone many changes, and new names have been introduced to reflect these changes. Some of the terms used in ancient palmistry were clearly derived from mythology and astrology; more recently, a new range of semiscientific terminology has been created. As a result, there may be two or even more names for the same thing. Traditional palmists are inclined to perpetuate the older names, while modern hand analysts tend to use the new terminology. It is difficult enough trying to learn something new without facing a confusion of terminology. For this reason a glossary seems not only desirable, but very necessary.

Air Hand In modern classification, one of the four hand types; it consists of a square palm and slightly longer fingers.

Allergy Line See Via Lascivia.

Angle of Dexterity The angle at the upper joint of the thumb.

Angle of Time The angle at the lower joint of the thumb.

Annular Finger The third or Apollo finger.

Apollo Line Also known as the line of Sun. It may start anywhere but leads to the Apollo mount.

Apollo Mount The fleshy prominence found under the third finger.

Arch Formation One of three types of finger settings on the top of the hand.

Arch Pattern One of the skin patterns.

Auricular Finger The little, or fourth finger.

Bar A short influence mark, an obstruction to a line.

Bracelets A small group of lines across the wrist just below the palm; also known as the rascettes.

Capillary Lines Skin pattern formation on palmar surface.

Career Line Another name for the fate line.

Chain A series of small islands that give a chaining effect to a line.

Chirognomy The study of hand shapes.

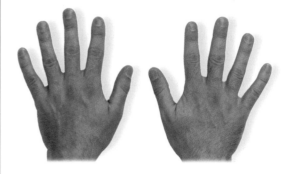

Chirology Modern term for palmistry. One who studies chirology is a chirologist.

Chiromancy Old name for the study of the lines of the hand. One who studies chiromancy is a chiromancer.

Composite Pattern One of the skin patterns.

Conic Traditional term, still widely used, for the round hand (as opposed to the square type).

Creative Curve The rounded outer edge of the percussion side of the hand.

Cross A small influence mark that may appear anywhere on a hand.

Dermatoglyphics The study of the skin ridge patterns in the hand.

Destiny Line Another name for the fate line.

Digital Mounts The fleshy prominences under each of the four fingers.

Duty Line Another name for the fate line.

Earth Hand In modern classification, one of the four hand types; it consists of a square palm and slightly shorter fingers.

Empty Hand A palm with very few visible lines.

Environment Line Another name for the fate line.

Family Ring A line, usually chained, found between the thumb and the mount of Venus.

Fate Line The traditional name for the line that runs from the base of the palm to the middle finger.

Fire Hand In modern classification, one of the four hand types; it consists of a rectangular palm and slightly shorter fingers.

Full Hand A palm full of lines that crisscross in all directions.

Girdle of Venus Two or three broken or chained lines found under the first, second, and third fingers.

Grille A series of small, close, vertical and horizontal influence lines that form a grille pattern on the surface of the palm.

Handprints A copy of the hand in print form.

Head Line Lower or proximal transverse line.

Health Line Another name for the Mercury line.

Heart Line Upper or distal transverse line.

Hepatica An ancient name for the Mercury line.

Hypothenar Eminence The mount of the Moon, or Luna mount, on the lower percussion side of the hand.

Imprints A more modern term for handprints.

Index Finger The first or Jupiter finger.

Influence Marks Any incidental lines or patterns that form anywhere on a hand.

Island Temporary division in a line.

Jupiter Finger The first or index finger.

Jupiter Mount The fleshy prominence under the first finger.

Knots Clearly defined bulges at the joints of the fingers.

Life Line The radial longitudinal line.

Liver Line An ancient name for the Mercury line.

Loop Pattern One of the skin patterns.

Lower Transverse Line Modern term for the head line.

Luna Mount Traditional name for the fleshy prominence on the lower percussion side of the hand; also called the mount of the Moon.

Lunula Modern term for the half-moon shape at the base of a fingernail.

Major Lines The four principal lines – life, head, heart, and fate.

Mars Line A secondary line usually found inside the life line.

Mars Negative Mount The fleshy prominence found on the percussion side of the hand, between the Luna and Mercury mounts.

Mars Positive Mount The fleshy prominence between the thumb and the Jupiter mounts.

Medical Stigmata Three or more short vertical lines on the Mercury mount, above the heart line

Medius Finger The Saturn or second finger.

Medius Mount The fleshy prominence under the second finger.

Mensal An ancient name for the head line.

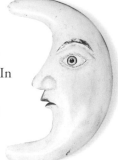

Mercury Line Another name for the health line. In ancient palmistry, it was known as the liver line or the hepatica.

Mercury Mount The fleshy prominence under the fourth finger.

Milieu Line A modern term for the line of fate.

Moons The small white half-moon shapes at the base of some fingernails.

Mounts Fleshy prominences on the palm. There are two types – the digital or finger mounts, and the palmar mounts.

Neptune Mount The fleshy prominence between the mounts of Luna and Venus.

Onychomancy An ancient name for the study of nails.

Palmar Ridges The "open" or "closed" skin pattern on the palmar surface.

Parathenar Area The middle of the palm, between the mounts of Luna and Venus.

Peacock's Eye A specifically shaped whorl usually on the third finger skin pattern.

Percussion The ulna, instinctive, or outer edge of a hand.

Phalange The section between two joints on a finger; each finger has three phalanges.

Plain of Mars Between the two mounts of Mars; also known as the zone of Mars.

Pollex An ancient name for the thumb.

Quadrangle The area between the heart and head lines; it is also known as the great quadrangle.

Radial The thumb or active side of the hand.

Radial Longitudinal Line The modern term for the life line.

Rascettes A small group of lines across the wrist just below the palm; also known as the bracelets.

Ridges Part of the capillary lines, or skin pattern.

Ring of Apollo A rarely seen line that circles the base of the third finger.

Ring of Saturn A line that circles the base of the medius.

Ring of Solomon A line usually placed high on the mount of Jupiter.

Saturn Finger The second or middle finger.

Saturn Mount The fleshy prominence under the second finger.

Sensitivity Pads Small dropletlike pads on the inner side of the top phalange of the fingers.

Simian Line A combined head and heart line.

Skin Pattern The ridges and furrows of the capillary lines.

Square A definite formation of lines that may appear on the hands or fingers.

Star A definite formation of lines that may appear on the hands or fingers.

Success Line Also called the Sun line.

Sydney Line A head line that completely crosses the palm from one side to the other.

Tented Arch One of the skin patterns.

Thenar Eminence The mount of Venus, the ball of the thumb.

Tri-radii A meeting point of types of skin pattern.

Triangle A definite formation of lines that may appear on hands or fingers.

Ulna The outer edge of the hand; also called the percussion or instinctive side.

Upper Transverse Line Modern term for the heart line.

Venus Mount The ball of the thumb.

Via Lascivia Traditional term for the allergy line, a small horizontal line that runs along the base of the Luna mount.

Water Hand In modern terminology, one of the four hand types, comprising a rectangular palm and slightly longer fingers.

Whorl One of the skin patterns.

Zone of Mars Modern term for the whole area of the lower, plain, and upper Mars.

FURTHER READING

* * * * * * * * * * * * * * * * * * *

ASANO, Hachiro,
HANDS (Japanese Handreading),
Japan Publications, Japan, 1985

BENHAM, William G.,
LAWS OF SCIENTIFIC
HANDREADING,
Rider, U.K., 1946

BRANDON-JONES, David,
PRACTICAL PALMISTRY,
Rider, U.K., 1981

CHEIRO,
YOU AND YOUR HAND,
Jarrolds, U.K., 1969 (revised edn.)

COMPTON, Vera,
PALMISTRY FOR EVERYMAN,
Duckworth, U.K., 1952

GAAFAR, MM.,
ILM-UL-KAFF (Egyptian
Handreading),
Taraporevala, India, 1959

HUTCHINSON, Beryl,
YOUR LIFE IN YOUR HANDS,
Neville Spearman, U.K., 1967

JACKSON, Dennis,
THE MODERN PALMIST,
The World's Work, U.K., 1953

JAQUIN, Noel,
THE HAND OF MAN,
Faber & Faber, U.K., 1933

MARJOLIN, Romayne and
REINER, Hannah,
POCKET PROPHECY: PALMISTRY,
Element Books, U.K., 1997

MEIER, Nellie,
LION'S PAWS,
Barrows Mussey, U.S.A., 1937

OXENFORD, Ina and
COSGRAVE, Anna,
LIFE STUDIES IN PALMISTRY,
Upcott Gill, U.K., 1899

REID, Lori,
ELEMENTS OF HANDREADING,
Element Books, U.K., 1994

ROBINSON, Mrs.,
THE GRAVEN PALM,
Edward Arnold, U.K., 1911

SORRELL, Walter,
THE HUMAN HAND,
Weidenfeld & Nicolson,
U.K., 1968

SPIER, Julius,
THE HANDS OF CHILDREN,
Routledge & Kegan Paul,
U.K., 1955

ST. HILL, Katherine,
BOOK OF THE HAND,
Rider & Co., U.K., 1910

TABORI, Paul,
BOOK OF THE HAND,
Chilton Company, U.S.A., 1962

WARREN-DAVIES, Dylan,
THE HAND REVEALS,
Element Books, U.K., 1993

WEST, Peter,
LIFELINES,
Quantum Press, U.K., 1998

INDEX

★ ★ ★ ★ ★ ★ ★ ★ ★ ★ ★ ★ ★ ★ ★ ★ ★ ★